CW00507123

THE HANDY GUIDE TO SOUTH AND WEST WALES

Everything You Need To Know
To See Amazing Welsh Sights

P. J. Wheeler

CONTENTS

MESSAGE FROM AUTHOR

This "Everything You Need To Know To See Amazing Welsh Sights" guide has unveiled many places that my Cardiff born and raised boyfriend had never heard of, making this a great companion for everyone - Welsh natives and visitors alike. I started collecting tidbits of travel knowledge in 2017, when I left America to live the nomadic lifestyle. On that first trip across the Atlantic Ocean, my second stop (after Iceland) was Wales - where I met my beau, which then resulted in numerous return trips over a three year period. We made a point in discovering every nook and cranny we could and I decided to write this book to help others visit Wales beyond the obvious sights with ease. Most of the places we were glad to see, but there were some that were a complete waste of time and money, or were not accessable due to being on private property. The last thing anyone wants to do is waste time seeing something that is less than impressive when you're only on vacation for a couple days or a week or two.

Sadly in 2020, Covid-19 put a damper on our adventuring, but thankfully by the time of the outbreak we had already been to the majority of sites around south and west Wales. Just like you - I do not have a team of professionals figuring this stuff out and sending me information to publish. As much that I would have liked to personally set foot at each location listed, the world dealing with the pandemic screwed up those plans. So, if I haven't been to a location that is listed, it is noted.

Living a nomadic lifestyle traveling from country to country, I am no stranger to finding my way around foreign lands and completely understand what information would be helpful, yet may not be readily available. Let's face it, a fantastic guidebook is worth it's weight in gold. So, if you want to get the most out of your vacation and money and you want to visit not-to-miss sights that are both, well known and barely known, then continue reading to plan your epic Welsh vacation.

INTRODUCTION

Wales may be a small country, but it's packed with plenty of historical interest and fun things to do. If you've been dreaming about seeing castles, you will not be disappointed. From imposing, strong structures that make bold statements to ruins that are in need of your imagination - all structures will bring wonder and awe. With so many historical assets within a concentrated area, it's easy to hop from castle to castle and also check out an abbey or cathedral along the way.

Historical monuments are not the only thing Wales has going for it, oh no, the rolling hillside and breathtaking coastline with its jagged limestone cliffs that soar above sandy beaches, will have you saying "wow". For those of you who are interested in learning about Welsh living and economics, from the past to the present, there are numerous museums - such as: The Big Pit Coal Museum, National Roman Legion and The St Fagans History Museum. Likewise, the wealthy citizens from days goneby have left their mark with stunning estates you can tour; or perhaps you had enough of history and are feeling adventurous, in that case, you can glide through the air on a zipline. Whatever you fancy, Wales offers an experience filled vacation that will last a lifetime and warrant a return.

With all that said, I have a confession, Wales was not at the top of my list when I first thought about seeing the world. But, it only took my first visit to be smittened. The downfall of the country is that it receives a lot of rain, but like the locals, I have learned to wear my rain gear, take my umbrella and enjoy all that is offered. So, now you might be wondering, how often does it rain? Well, if there isn't rainfall within a three week period during the summer the citizens are concerned about drought. Hopefully, that statement gives you enough insight.

In this guide you will find must-see sights and a heads-up to those I believe will be a waste of your time - not every castle is worth the drive or is accessable. I have been to nearly everywhere listed in this guide book, but if I have not been there personally I have indicated as such. Site details included: a brief summary, admission fee (at time of print), hours open, parking information, address, website, how to get there from Cardiff City Center - by car, train and bus, if dogs are allowed, services available and a list of nearby sights. Generally, the majority of sites do not allow drones.

Renting a car is the easiest and best way to get around Wales and the rest of the United Kingdom. With that said, I personally have not driven in the UK, thankfully, my Welsh guy is happy to be my chauffeur. If you are traveling with someone - I highly suggest choosing the best navigator, this will help make the driving task easier for the one behind the wheel. One of the best inventions we have nowadays is the GPS, yet, while driving in a foreign country it is not easy to understand what is being said and where to go, especially while driving on the opposite side of the street than what you are used to. While I was in Scotland with an American friend I had her drive while I navigated and it worked out great; if we switched roles it would not have gone as well - her navigation skills are not as strong as mine. Sure, she was completely nervous behind the wheel, but my calm and precise directions made our journey across country less stressful - for both of us.

Once you are out of the city, the motorway and country roads are pretty easy to maneuver so you can relax a bit, just mind your speed. Unlike in America where you will see police watching the roadways, the United Kingdom has speed cameras set in place. The national speed limit is 70 mph on motorways and 60 mph on single-carriageways, and oddly, it's even the speed limit on the one-lane country roads - which is indicated by a sign that is a plain white circle with a black diagonal stripe. It is literally impossible to get to such speed on the majority of country lanes - imagine driving with blinders on and only being able to see a few feet ahead; the hedge-lined roads are curvy and barely wide enough for one vehicle. When you come head to head with an oncoming car, it will be the person closest to a pull out that will be the one who is expected to move aside or backup - unless there is more than one car in the line-up. Depending on who you come up against, you might be expected to back up twenty feet or more to allow them to squeeze past. If you are in a rental car, you might want bring in your side mirror, so it isn't hit by the passing vehicle - and always bring the side mirror inward when you park for the same reason.

Summertime is the best time of year to get the most out of your day, with the sunrising by 5am and sunset around 9pm - allowing plenty of time for a fully-packed outing. Winter has about eight hours of daylight - in January it is nearly dark by 4pm. With that said, Wales is a country that is great to visit anytime of the year, just dress appropriately and be sure to check winter hour schedules (which are listed in this guide).

Making Cardiff your vacation homebase will allow visiting two to four sights on any given day. The months where the days are longer you can pack in seven or eight - making a loop back to your accomodations. For those of you who want to stay in different towns along the way - having a rental car will make your holiday travels easier, not only because it takes twice as long to get to where you are going by public transportation, but there are also many cool things that are nearly impossible to see without a car. My directions on how to get somewhere does include getting around by train and bus for those who will not be renting a vehicle; there are many different routes to take, not just what I listed. If you are going to a populated town, you'll find your way easy enough - yet, off-the-beaten-path locations will be more difficult and will involve walking the rest of the way or calling an Uber or taxi. I included train and bus directions just to give you an idea of what kind of hoops you are going to have to jump through; yes, there are more details involved, but it's not impossible to get where you want to go.

It is important to note that as of 2020, the road directly in front of Cardiff Castle has been closed off to vehicles and is now a pedestrian zone. A taxi area has been put in place, which you can locate at the end of the castle and Bute Park entrance.

Train travel is expensive within the United Kingdom and as much as I have wanted to travel by train, I have not. There are two nationwide bus companies - National Express and MegaBus. I have not used MegaBus except while I was in Canada, which I did have a good experience. My choice for public transportation between London airports or Bristol airport and Cardiff is always with National Express. Yes, even with having a boyfriend that lives only a few hours away, I still take the bus to and from the airport when I fly out of London - it saves him time and cost of fuel runs about double of the bus fare. Taking the bus is extremely easy and it is cheaper. A one-way ticket between Cardiff and London cost between £13- £28 when pre-booked online and under £10 between Cardiff and Bristol. One time I had to fly into Heathrow and my beau could not pick me up, so I bought my bus ticket upon landing and I had to pay £60 - ouch! It is around a 5-hour bus ride from London to Cardiff - driving yourself will take about 2.5 to 3 hours - of course, it all depends on time of day. If you are interested in taking the bus, here is a money saving tip: when you purchase your ticket online there is no need to pick a seat on the website, no one does this - just board and sit wherever you like. This will save you the "pick-your-seat" fee.

If you are thinking about purchasing a Cadw Explorer Pass, you are going to have to plan to visit more than three or four accepted sites that have an entrance fee to off-set your pass cost. Visiting many Cadw sites with the pass in hand may save money, but then again, you can be flushing it down the drain too - because the majority of ruins are free. I have included a Cadw site list and I suggest you visit their website, cadw.gov.wales, to download a touring map for planning while you are at home - then when are in Wales grab a free printed map at your first destination.

If you own a phone that is locked, you can skip this part, since you are unable to remove your Sim card. I recommend getting yourself a Vodafone Sim card. The company offers enough options to get you through your vacation - either with pre-paid minutes or Big Value Bundle. I tend to get by just fine using pre-paid minutes. After spending £1 (about 30mb of usage - via messsenger, online, email) the company sends you a text saying you now have 500mb to use for the rest of the day - ending at midnight. If you do not plan on using your phone much, pre-paid is a great way to have access to the internet, Uber, Facetime, GPS, social media and email - and if you are like me, you will still have enough data remaining to stream one short television episode. The Big Value Bundles come in £10 (3gb), £20 (10gb) and £30 (20gb), and are good for 29 days or until you use up the agreed data. I personally have found that using the pre-paid is better than buying a £10 BVB, you can make it last longer - the pre-credit remains in your account until you have used it all, regardless if it is within 4 days or 4 years, it does not expire. If you will be streaming movies and uploading a ton of photos to social media daily, without using your accomodations Wifi, then I suggest going for the £30 Big Value Bundle. To purchase your Sim card you have to go into a Vodafone outlet store and provide your passport information to purchase a plan, even for pre-paid minutes and Vodafone ONLY accepts credit cards in their stores. To add more credit you can buy a "top-up" voucher at most gas stations where paying with cash is acceptable; to add the voucher amount to your phone is easy, dial 2345 from your mobile phone and chose whatever option you would like: pre-paid or bundle. Of course, you can go with another carrier: EE or o2, which might be better. I use Vodafone, therefore I have given their services as an example.

Cardiff is easy to get around by public transportation - bus and train are both available. I have not taken the train when I go into city center, but the bus runs pretty much on schedule and tickets cost £2 one-way or £3.80 for a daily pass. You purchase your bus ticket on the bus and you need the exact amount - no change is given back; you drop your coins into a machine next to the driver and tell him if you want a single ride or daily pass - he will hand you the ticket.

For those of you who smoke, all Burial Chambers, Castles, Gardens, Heritage Homes, Museums, Theatres, Steam Trains and everything else listed in this guide (and not listed), except public beaches - do not allow smoking on property - including vapes.

Now that you have the low-down on what to expect and those details you might of had questions about - let us move forward to the sights so you can start the fun part in planning.

BEACHES

T he Welsh coastline is spectacular! Even if you are not a beach-goer it is worthy of a trip to the coast just to see the jagged limestones and sheer cliffs. An easy to walk coastal route runs along the whole stretch of Wales, but be cautious of how close you are from the edge while walking the ridge - landslides happen often.

The majority of beaches are sandy, yet there are a few that are pebble. I didn't think I would like a pebble beach, but they do have the bonus of not having sand sticking to your skin and clothing.

Dunraven Bay at Southerndown

Dunraven Bay - one of the most beautiful beaches near Cardiff, less than an hours drive away - is enjoyable for those who love the beach and for those who do not. The coastal path is accessible in both directions from the beach, plus historical ruins are located within a few minutes walk.

On the outskirts of Southerdown before descending the hill to the beach, there is a metered car park, which may be a cheaper choice than if you drive down to the parking lot - both times I've been there the machine was out-of-order; if this area is full or you want to be closer, the "official" parking lot down the hill has a daily fee of £5.

If hiking is more your style than frolicking in the surf or sunbathing, follow the path to the fortress wall and wander within - soon you will discover the hidden garden. A number of path options veer off heading north, south and east. Exiting south brings you to the path that takes you along the lands edge. This is a place known for people jumping to their death and I can see how it can happen accidently too. There are no guard rails in place, so keep a good distance from the edge - the cliffs are very unstable and landslides do occur. Of course, keep a hand on your children and pets on a leash; it would make a very bad day if Fido went after the ball in the wrong direction.

You have the option of following a couple trails that go through farmland or you can turn back and walk the tree-lined path. I suggest you turn back and take the path, on the left, and find the gate. Go through the gate! The first time I went to Dunraven there was a couple that were standing in front of the gate and eyeing the pathway that went up the hill through the trees - debating if they should enter. She wanted to, but her husband did not. His explaination was "the leaves do not look like they have been walked on," so they chose not to explore. We had a good laugh at their lack of adventure, especially when we emerged from the trees and saw the view - the coastline is nothing less than magnificent. If a gate is not locked, it is okay to enter - unless otherwise posted.

- Cost: Free
- Parking: £5 at car park - or park up top of hill at pay and display
- Address: Southerndown, Bridgend, CF32 0RP
- Website: visitthevale.com

How to get there:

- Car: A470 and M4 from Cardiff. From M4 take A473 in Pencoed to Southerndown. Continue on A473. Turn right onto Southerndown Rd/B4524 then left staying on B4524. Follow to Dunraven Bay in Vale of Glamorgan.

- *Alternative route from Cardiff- A4232, at roundabout, take 2nd exit, A48. Continue onward, left onto B4524. Turn right onto Southerndown Rd/B4524 then left staying on B4524

- Estimated Travel Time: 40 minutes

- Train and Bus: Cardiff Central towards Carmarthen (20 minutes, non-stop), exit at Pen-y-Bont/Bridgend, walk about 2 minutes to Station Hill, take bus line 303 Llantwit Major (20 minutes/ 15 stops) to Three Golden Cups. Walk about 10 minutes to Dunraven Bay.

- Estimated Travel Time: 1 hour 15 minutes to 1 hour 50 minutes

- Bus: National Express, Sophia Gardens, Cardiff Coach Station to Bridgend (£4.10 /30 - 40 minute journey). From Bridgend take bus line 303 Llantwit Major from Ewenny Road to Three Golden Cups then walk about 10 minutes to Dunraven Bay.

- Estimated Travel Time: 1 hour 20 minutes

Services

- Dogs allowed

- Snack bar
- Toilets

Nearby: Ewenny Priory (11 min/ 4.1 miles away), Ogmore Castle (6 mins/ 2.1 miles), Penarth Pier (38 mins/ 26 miles)

Oxwich Bay Beach

Not the best beach, but it'll do - that is, if you do not mind ragworms. What is a ragworm? A disgusting centipede-looking-type worm that coil up on top of the sand. They do have the capacity to bite and are poisonous - I walked by hundreds of them during my low-tide stroll.

I also came across a huge Barrell Jelly Fish and a Blue Jelly Fish, both dead on the sand - both pack a punch with their stingers, so enter the water at your own risk.

- Cost: Free
- Parking: £5 in the parking lot - I recommend saving your cash and park for free on a side street.
- Address: Oxwich, Swansea, SA3 1LS
- Website: visitwales.com

How to get there:

- Car: M4 from A470/Cardiff. Follow on

M4 until junction 42, exit onto A483 towards Swansea/Abertawe - A483 continue onto Quay Parade/A4067, turn right onto Mayals Rd/B4436 (bypassing The Mumbles - which is worthy of a visit), turn right onto Vennaway Ln/B4436 then left onto A4118 then turn left again to Oxwich Beach

- Estimated Travel Time: 1 hour 20 minutes

- Train and Bus: Cardiff Central to Swansea - then from Bus Station, bus line 118 Rhossili (20 minutes/ 15 stops), exit Gower Road, take bus line 117 Scurlage (25 minutes/ 15 stops) to Oxwich Cross and walk about 10 minutes to Oxwich Bay Beach

- Estimated Travel Time: 3 hours

- Bus: National Express from Sofia Gardens, Cardiff to Swansea (£5.20 - £5.50) then from Swansea Bus Station bus line 118 Rhossili (20 minutes/ 15 stops), exit Gower Road, take bus line 117 Scurlage (25 minutes/ 15 stops) to Oxwich Cross and walk about 10 minutes to Oxwich Bay Beach

- Estimated Travel Time: 3 hours

Services

- Dogs allowed
- Snack bar
- Toilets

Nearby: Oystermouth Castle (23 mins/ 10 miles away) Swansea Museum (27 min/ 12 miles away)

Presipe Beach

A hidden beach with golden sand that is only accessible by coastal path and stairs. It is located between Manorbier Bay and Skrinkle Haven Beach - separated by a Royal Artillery Range (the coastal trail will take you inland and around the range).

At the car park below Manorbier Castle - you will need to take the trail on the left side of the bay that follows the coastline. It's an easy 40 minute walk with spectacular views of the rugged coastline; actually, if you do not stop to take photos every so many feet like I do, the walk is probably less than 30 minutes. The only downfall is that you will have to descend steps that are carved out of earth with timber to get down to the beach. I didn't go down them, but the website below states there's 160 steps. When you come around the bend and you first see the beach the steps are not visable, keep walking and you will come to them shortly before you reach the gate that enters farmland.

Be sure to check tide chart before heading to the beach and beware of undertow. And as always, let's all do our part in keeping our planet clean - please pack out what you packed in.

- Cost: Free
- Parking: Pay and display car park at the beach located below Manorbier Castle - Free parking during winter
- Address: Coastal path, Manorbier, SA70 7SZ
- Website: thebeachguide.co.uk

How to get there:

- Walk: Coastal path from Manorbier

Services

- Dogs allowed
- No toilets at beach, but are available at the parking lot

Nearby: Manorbier Castle (at parking location) and Lamphey Bishops Palace (12 mins/ 4.3 miles away)

Rhossili Bay Beach

If you are into surfing this is the place! This beach is popular with the pro's and newbies. For those of you who have wanted to learn, there are surf schools (see *Websites Recommended).

Sand dunes seperate the parking area from the coast, it's an easy, well beaten path; it only takes a few minutes to trek over them.

During low tide, the skeletal remains of the ship-wrecked vesssel Helvetia can be seen, located on the beach. Also during low tide there is a causeway over to Worms Head, be sure to check tidal charts; you do not want to be stuck when the tide rolls back in.

Rhossili beach is three miles long and has been voted Wales best beach.

The chapter photo is this beach.

- Cost: Free
- Parking: Free
- Address: Hillend Gower, SA3 1PP, Grid ref: SS 4142 8858
- Website: thebeachguide.co.uk
- Dogs allowed
- No toilets at beach, but are available at parking area

How to get there:

- Walk: Coastal path
- Car: Take the M4 out of Cardiff towards Swansea. M4 to Fabian Way/A483 then B4436 to A4118 to B4247. You will be driving on a one-lane country road for awhile, just keep driving. There are no signs indicating there is

a beach up ahead, or non that we saw. Eventually you will come to the end of the road, which is where you want to be.

Skrinkle Haven Beach & Church Doors Beach

These two beaches are connected during low tide, which means that they are separated when the tide comes in. Cement and metal stairs lead to Church Doors Beach, if you have the knees for it - there are 140 steps. The only way down to Skrinkle Haven is by walking down the limestone ridge. I have not been to these beaches yet.

Check tide chart! Pay attention to the incoming tide when you're basking on the sands - you don't want to get trapped on Skrinkle Haven Beach.

Keep on the coastal path, heading west, and you will come to Presipe Beach - after the Royal Artillery Range.

- Cost: Free
- Parking: Car park with pay and display
- Address: Coastal path, SA70 7SH - Manorbier/ Tenby
- Website: thebeachguide.co.uk

How to get there:

- Walk: Coastal path

- Bus: The 349 bus from Tenby makes stops at: Skrinkle Estate and Manorbier House - making it easy to get to Skrinkle and Church Doors beach in and Presipe near Manorbier

Services

- Dogs allowed
- No Toilets at beach, but are available at car park

Nearby: Tenby (12 mins/ 5.7 miles), Manorbier Castle (5 mins/ 1.2 miles), Lamphey Bishops Palace (12 mins/ 4.3 miles away)

BURIAL
CHAMBERS

Everytime I visit a burial chamber I stand in wonder and you will too. It is not necessary to visit them all, but I do suggest you stop by one or two to marvel at the accomplishment. Standing stones and burial chambers were not built to impress, but they are an attraction not to be missed.

Carreg Coetan Arthur Burial Chamber

While it is a small burial chamber, it is said to have a link to the legendary King Arthur. This site isn't worth going out of your way: I included Pentre Ifan Burial Chamber, St. Dogmaels Abbey and a visit to the town of Fishguard.

- Cost: Free
- Parking: No onsite parking available. Site is located on private drive, but there is street parking available on a side street just across the way.

- Open: 10am - 4pm - located a few feet away from gate, so no entry needed to see it, if gate happens to be locked

- Address: 1 Carreg Coetan, Newport, SA42 0LT

- Website: cadw.gov.wales

How to get there:

- Car: M4 to Carmarthen, then continue on B4298 and the A47 to Carreg Coetan

- Estimated travel time: 2 hours 10 minutes

- Train: Cardiff Central to Milford Haven (2h 25min/ 12 stops), exit Haverfordwest and walk to Railway Station bus stop. Take T5

TranwsCymru/Aberystwyth (1h 15min/ 22 stops) exit Golden Lion Hotel - walk about 3 minutes - east along East St/A487 towards Bromeddyg, turn left onto Feidr Pen-y-Bont and left on Carreg Coetan - taking care walking on the road to destination

- Estimated travel time: 4 hours

- Bus: National Express, Sophia Gardens, Cardiff to Steynton for Milford Haven (£15 - £20/ 3.5 - 4.5hours) in Steynton, take the 302/Withybush (26 min/ 13 stops), exit at Fishguard Road then take T5 TrawsCymru/ Aberystwyth (50 min/ 20 stops) Golden Lion Hotel then walk 3 minutes to destination

- Estimated travel time: 6 hours

Services

- Dogs allowed

- No drones

- No services

Nearby: Pentre Ifan Burial Chamber (2.82 miles away), St Dogmaels Abbey (Castle 7.63 miles away), Cilgerran (8.67 miles away)

Pentre Ifan Burial Chamber

I was in utter awe when I saw the top stone balanced upon the tips of four 6ft vertical stones. Even though it only takes a couple of minutes to admire this ancient site - it is worth seeing.

The chapter photo is this burial chamber.

- Cost: Free
- Parking: Free, there is enough space available near gate for street parking
- Open: Year-round, 10am - 4pm, with the exemption of December 24, 25 and 26 and January 1
- Address: Nevern, Crymych, SA41 3TZ
- Website: cadw.gov.wales

How to get there:

- Car: M4 to Bridgend, continue 46 miles, at 2nd roundabout exit onto A48, keep on A48 until A40 exit, turn right onto B4298 follow to A478, take left onto B4329 to destination
- Estimated travel time: 2 hours

Services

- Dogs not allowed
- No drones
- No services

Nearby: Carreg-Coetan Arthur Burial Chamber (2.82 miles away), Castell Henllys Iron Age Village (3.6 miles away), St Dogmaels Abbey and Coach House (6.82 miles away), Cilgerran Castle (7.04 miles away), Fishguard (11 miles away)

St. Lythan's Burial Chamber

It will only take a minute to see this attraction, but it's right around the corner from Dyffryn Gardens, so you might as well stop - that is if you have your own car, it's not worth the effort otherwise.

The stones are set in a farmers field, only a few feet from the gate. Crank the handle on the information box to hear a story about the stones.

- Cost: Free
- Parking: Free on street
- Address: Carreg Coetan, SA42 0LT
- Website: cadw.gov.wales

How to get there:

- Car: From Cardiff take Penarth Rd/A4160 continue on Penarth Rd/A4160. Turn right onto Hadfield Rd and A4232 to St Lythans Rd in Wenvoe. There is an information plaque and gate indicating the entrance.
- Estimated Travel Time: 25 minutes

Services

- Dogs not allowed
- No drone
- No services

Nearby: Castell Coch (6.67 miles), Dyffryn Gardens and Tinkinswood Burial Chamber (.83 miles) and Old Beaupre' Castle (5.51 miles)

Tinkinswood Burial Chamber

There's a little more walking involved to get to the chambers than nearby St. Lythan's, but it is only about five minutes and it is an easy trek across a farmers field. This chamber is a decent size, about three times the size of St Lythan's.

You will want to make sure to wear appropriate footwear; I went here during winter and even though it had not rained for a few days, the ground was muddy around the access gates.

- Cost: Free
- Parking: Free on street
- Address: Dyffryn Lane, Cardiff, CF5 6S
- Website: cadw.gov.wales

How to get there:

- Car: Penarth Rd/A4160 take A4232 and A48 to Dyffryn Ln in Saint Nicholas
- Bus: Central Station JN take bus line X2 Porthcawl (23 minutes/ 5 stops) to St. Nicholas then walk about 14 minutes to Dyffryn Lane

Services

- Dogs not allowed
- No drones
- No services

Nearby: Dyffryn Gardens, St. Lythans Burial Chamber and Old Beaupre' Castle (see St. Lythans above for distance between sites). If you are traveling by bus, you can walk to Dyffryn Gardens then exit the estate through the back entrance to St Lythans Burial Chamber - take care walking if you do, these sights are located on narrow country lanes without sidewalks. St Lythans Burial Chamber is not far down the road, take a right out of property, turning left at the end of the lane and then walking about 150 feet. Then on your way back to town, follow your footsteps back to Dyffryn Gardens, but instead of going into the estate, keep walking and you will come to Tinkinswood Burial Chamber shortly.

CASTLES

From imposing structures that still today make bold statements to bits of ruins that induce your imagination - the Castles of Wales are sure to have your jaw drop in awe. Once upon a time, the land was saturated with castles - in fact, 600 dotted the Welsh landscape; nowadays only 100 remain standing. Even with the majority no longer existing, it's easy to hop from one to another, plus check out a nearby abbey or cathedral for a stellar day out.

Three "must-see" castles that are easy to reach while staying in the capital city are: Cardiff Castle, Castell Coch and Caerphilly. The grand interiors of Cardiff Castle and Castle Coch will have you wishing you called them home and even though Caerphilly is a ruin - it is fantastic and will definitely satisfy your castle craving. I have been inside nearly every castle within a two and a half hour drive from Cardiff and I can say, after you've seen three or four - you will notice that there is not much change from one to another; the exceptions are the first two I mentioned.

If you are in Wales for a long period, I highly recommend looking into purchasing a Cadw Explorer Pass. The thing is though, not every castle qualifies - such as Cardiff Castle - and many properties are free. Yet, if you plan on visiting Caerphilly Castle, Castell Coch and Chepstow Castle - you just paid for your 3-day pass.

CadwExplorer Passes

The pass offers great flexiblity in terms of usage; the 3-day pass can be used within a 7-day period.

The 7-day pass is valid for a 14-day period. My recommendation is to look at the list below and mark the sights that you will be visiting, then decide if purchasing a pass is in your best interest - as I previously mentioned, numerous Cadw sights are free; this list features only properties that charge admission.

Cost: **3-Day Pass**: Single £23.10, Two Adults £35.70, Family £47.25

7-Day Pass: Single £33.60, Two Adults £53.55, Family £65.10

- Family pass consist of: 2 adults and up to 3 children under 18

- St David's Day - free entry to Cadw sites in Wales, you must pre-book your ticket on the cadw website for Castell Coch, I am unsure about other attractions - cadw.gov.wales.

The historical listings below: accept and sell Explorer Passes (unless noted). The list includes properties in North and South Wales; I have noted the sights located in North Wales.

- Beaumaris Castle - North Wales

- Blaenavon Ironworks

- Carreg Cennen Castle (*accepts/ does not sell passes)

- Caernarfon Castle - North Wales

- Caerphilly Castle
- Castell Coch
- Chepstow Castle
- Cilgerran Castle
- Conwy Castle - North Wales
- Criccieth Castle - North Wales
- Denbigh Castle - North Wales
- Dolwyddelan (*accepts/ does not sell passes) - North Wales
- Harlech Castle - North Wales
- Kidwelly Castle
- Laugharne Castle
- Margam Stones Museum (*accepts/ does not sell passes)
- Oxwich Castle
- Plas Mawr Elizabethan Town House - North Wales
- Raglan Castle
- Rhuddlan Castle - North Wales
- Rug Chapel - North Wales
- Strata Florida Abbey - North Wales
- St Davids Bishop's Palace
- Tintern Abbey

- Tretower Court and Castle
- Valle Crucis Abbey - North Wales
- Weobley Castle (*accepts/ does not sell passes)

Caerphilly Castle

The second largest intact castle in the United Kingdom, Caerphilly is definitely worth a visit. Gilbert de Clare commissioned this castle and had it built with not just one motte, but two, with extra security of having drawbridges not just outside the walls but inside too - making this castle very impressive.

Today, one of the towers leans more than the Leaning Tower of Pisa in Italy and offers a fun photo op with a knight statue posed to look like he is holding up the tower.

Visiting the castle will take a few hours, pack a picnic and enjoy your meal while sitting in the courtyard.

Caerphilly Castle has been used in the BBC series *Merlin*

- Cadw: Yes
- Cost: Adults £9.40, Kids (5-17) £5.60, Family £26.20, Seniors £7.50
- Parking: Free on street

- Open: 9am - 5pm
- Address: Castle Street, Caerphilly, CF83 1JD
- Website: cadw.gov.wales

How to get there:

- Car: Take the A470 from Cardiff City Center - head north on Kingsway/A4161, continue onto North Rd/A470, slight left onto Caerphilly Rd/A469, then turn onto B4263
- Estimated Travel Time: 20 minutes
- Train: Cardiff Central to Caerphilly, walk about 10 minutes to castle
- Estimated Travel Time: 30 minutes
- Bus: Philharmonic JP - bus line 26 gold Blackwood, ride for 39 minutes/ 29 stops, exit Castle Court Bandstand then walk about 4 minutes to the castle
- Estimated Travel Time: 45 minutes
- Uber: From downtown Cardiff, £12 - £20+

Services

- Dogs allowed on ground floors
- No drones
- Cafe
- Gift shop
- Toilets

Nearby: Castell Coch (12 min/ 4 miles away), Llandaff Cathedral (18 min/ 7 miles away). Roman Baths - Amphitheater & Roman Legion (31 min/ 15 miles away)

I highly recommend Caerphilly Castle

Caldicot Castle

This restored Norman castle ended up being more enjoyable visiting than I anticipated. It isn't fancy by any means, but what it lacks in "wow", they have made up for by adding some interesting historical furnishings and facts. During the self-guided tour, I learned that Thomas of Woodstock, son of Edward III, called this castle home; later he was imprisoned for conspiracy against his nephew, King Richard II.

People have used this dwelling for 800 years and besides being a fortress and manor house to some prestigious owners, the post-war WWII sections were transformed into apartments.

- Cost: Free
- Parking: Free
- Open: April to October 11am - 4pm Tuesday to Sunday - Closed on Mondays (except Bank Holidays)
- Address: Church Rd, Caldicot, NP26 4HU

How to get there:

- Car: M4 to A48 - In Cardiff, take M4 to A48 in Newport. Exit 24 on the M4, continue on A48 to the castle

- Estimated travel time: 40 - 50 minutes

- Train and bus: Cardiff Central to Newport, walk about 6 minutes to Newport Friars Walk and take X74 Chepstow ride for 49 minutes/ 24 stops, exit at Caldicot Cross and walk about 8 minutes to the castle

- Estimated travel time: 1 hour 30 minutes

- Bus: Cardiff to Newport - Newport to Chepstow, take bus line 74 Chepstow and exit at Caldicot Cross, then walk about 8 minutes to the castle.

- Estimated travel time: 2 hours 40 minutes

Services

- Dogs allowed ground floor

- No drones

- Toilets

Nearby: Chepstow Castle (14 min/ 6.4 miles away), Dewstow Gardens and Grotto (7 min/ 2.2 miles away), Roman Baths - Amphitheater & Roman Legion (24 min/ 12 miles away), Castell Coch 38 min/ 27 miles away), Big Pit (44 min/ 27 miles away)

Cardiff Castle

Cardiff Castle, right in the heart of the city, dates back 2000 years. This prime real estate was first claimed by the Romans during Emperor Nero's reign and the remains of the Roman built wall are visible. In the 11th century, the Normans made claim and built a wooden Keep, known as a "shell keep", which was later replaced with rock.

In the 19th century, the Bute family took possession and transformed the property into a fairytale palace featuring an astrology room that contains all twelve zodiac signs and phases of the sun and moon - in each season. The nursery is decorated with Aesop's beloved storybook characters and even features an "invisable man" - if you look closely at the tree you can see his outline. The other must-see room is the Arabic room, decorated in gold, is truly jaw-dropping. The first time I took the tour I was too busy concentrating on photography, which lead me to taking the tour again so I could pay attention to what the tour guide was explaining. Each room has an interesting tale behind it and worth hearing.

During WWII the outer wall tunnel provided safety to the locals during air raids. Today you can venture the tunnel and read antique signs promoting women being recruited to work in the factories, lights-out protocol and conserving food.

Cardiff Castle has been used in BBC hits: *Doctor Who*, *Sherlock*, *Torchwood* and *The Sarah Jane Adventures*. The castle offers a film location tour for an additional price. I have not taken the film tour, but I know the library has been used in the tv shows.

Check the website for activities, such as - jousting events and comedy shows that take place within the castle walls.

- Cadw: No
- Cost: Adults £13.50, Kids (5-16) £9.50, Seniors and Students £11.50,   Family ticket consist of 2 adults and 2 children: Family £39, Senior Family £36, additional children £5.50 each
- Admission includes: Castle grounds, apartments, Norman Keep, wartime tunnels, Cardiff Castle Museum of Welsh Soldiers and a free audio guide.
- Upgrade your ticket to include a house tour for £3.75 - it is well worth the extra cost! There are additional add-ons, check website for details.
- Parking: Nearby pay and display parking lot or parking garage
- Open: March - October, 9am - 6pm, November - February, 9am - 5pm

- Address: Cardiff City
- Website: cardiffcastle.com

Services

- Dogs not allowed, with exception to guide dogs
- No drones
- Cafe
- Gift Shop
- Toilets

Nearby: Bute Park (next to property), River Taff (next to property), Insole Court (7 min/ 2.4 miles away), Llandaff Cathedral (8 min/ 2.2 miles away), Cardiff Bay (11 min/ 3.2 miles away), St Fagan's National Museum (14 min/ 6.6 miles away), Castell Coch (16 min/ 5.7 miles away), Caerphilly Castle (19 min/ 7.9 miles away)

I highly recommend Cardiff Castle and tour

Carreg Cennen Castle

According to *Countryfile* magazine, "Carreg Cennen is the most romantic castle in Wales". I do not agree - perhaps they have only seen a couple of castles to make this statement. Yes, as they mention it has a great view, but so do many others - like the other two I visited on the same day

(Dinefwr and Dryslwyn).

The area around the castle has a nice walking path that leads through sheep pastures and woodlands to get to the castle. The owners of the working farm have asked visitors to not make contact with livestock - sheep and horses. There is a souvenir shop and tearoom, purchase your tickets inside the tearoom before heading up the hill; then at the ticket booth below the castle, they will collect your ticket and allow entry.

Near the ticket booth there is a gate that leads to a trail through the woodland and hills - if you have time, and fancy a hike, take it - the trail is free.

Audio tour is available.

- Cadw: Yes
- Cost: Adults £5.50, Junior £3.50 (ages 5 - 17), Family £16.00 (2 adults/3 kids), Armed Forces & Veterans £3.50, Seniors (aged 65+) £4.50
- Open: April - October 9am - 6pm, November - March 9:30am - 4:30pm, Closed Christmas Day
- Parking: Free parking - car park is locked at 6pm
- Address: Trapp, Llandeilo SA19 6UA
- Website: cadw.gov.wales

How to get there:

- Car: M4, continue to A483 to the castle
- Estimated travel time: 1 hour 30 minutes
- Train: Cardiff Central - Millford Haven to Swansea (51 mins/ 4 stops), Swansea - Llandovery to Llandeilo (56 mins/ 9 stops) - then walk 1hr 45 minutes to destination -or, perhaps Uber is available in Llandeilo. The walk to the castle is on a one lane road, it's dangerous enough being in a car with all the blind corners. I cannot recommend walking on this road.
- Estimated travel tiime: 1 hour 55 minutes, Plus 1 hour and 45 minutes walking time
- Bus: From Cardiff - Canal Street JF - X10 bus towards Swansea, then the X13 Cymru Clipper towards Llandeilo - then walk 1 hour 45 minutes to destination. Personally, I cannot recommend going by bus (or train); not only will it take a long time to walk from the nearest town, but it's a dangerous road to walk on to destination.
- Estimated travel time: 2 hour 30 minutes, Plus 1 hour and 45 minutes walking time
- Bike: NCN Route #47 (9 miles)

Services
- Dogs allowed
- No drones

- Cafe
- Gift shop
- Toilets
- Hiking trail access

Nearby: National Showcaves and Dinosaur Park (18 min/ 5.8 miles away), Dinefwr Castle & Newton House (17 min /5.7 miles), Aberglasney Gardens (18 miles away), Dryslwyn Castle (19 min/ 9.3 miles away), Paxton's Tower (23 min/ 11 miles away), National Botanic Gardens (23 min/ 11 miles away)

Cardigan Castle

Covid-19 restrictions and pouring rain put a damper on visiting the town and it's castle, but, driving through to check it out intrigued my beau and I enough to mark it as a place we must return for an overnight stay. For me, Cardigan tics all the boxes of an idyllic Welsh town.

Since we did not physically leave our vehicle, I will say that "I have not visited here yet."

- Cadw: No
- Cost: Adults £6, Children £3 (aged 3-16), Family £15

 Tickets allow entry for 12 months

- Open: 10am - 4pm everyday

- Parking: Not listed, I presume there is a car park
- Address: Green Street, Cardigan, SA43 1JA
- Website: cardigancastle.com

How to get there:

- Car: M4 and A48 to B4298 in Carmarthenshire. Continue on B4298, take A478 to High Street in Cardigan
- Estimated travel time: 2 hour 6 minutes
- Train: Cardiff Central towards Milford Haven exit in Clunderwen (2h 13 min/ 10 stops) - walk about 1 minute to War Memorial and take bus 430/Cardigan (52 min/ 25 stops) exit Grosvenor Hill walk to castle
- Estimated travel time: 4 hours
- Bus: From Swansea walk about 2 minutes to High Street Station take T1s TrawsCymru/ Carmarthen (47 minutes/ 4 stops) Bus Station take the 460 TrawsCymru Connection/Cardigan (1h 29 mins/ 53 stops), exit Finch Square A, walk about 4 minutes to destination
- Estimated travel time: 4 hours

Services

- Dogs allowed, £1 per dog with maximum 2 dogs per visitor
- No drones

- Cafe
- Gift Shop

Nearby: St Dogmaels Abbey (4 mins/ 1.1 miles), Cilgerran (7 mins/ 3.2 miles), Pentre Ifan Burial Chamber (19 mins/ 10 miles away)

Carew Castle and Tidal Mill

An absolute delightful castle and a must-visit, you will want to fit it into your schedule.

Grand castles have grand stories and Carew is no exception. During your self-guided tour, you will learn about Princess Nest's ghost. It is said to haunt the castle. Princess Nest, the daughter of Rhys ap Tewdwr, a Celtic king, married Gerald de Windsor the owner of Carew. Like many marriages in that era, this union was to increase Tewdwr's rule over the locals. The story goes to say that one day: Welsh Prince Owain stormed the castle - this act lead Gerald to run to the loo to escape down the toilet shaft to safety, resulting in the capture of Princess Nest. Not only did Gerald get gunk on his face from his means of escape, but apparently Princess Nest didn't mind Prince Owain; she stayed with him for quite some time and the two produced a couple of kids.

Also on the property is the only restored Tidal Mill, which is easily accessible by trail along Mill-pond from the castle. It makes a nice stroll on a sunny day.

There is a tearoom and souvenir shop - by the way, castles and museums sell the best souvenirs. If you see something you like, buy it - because chances are low you will come across it again.

- Cadw: No
- Cost: Adults £5, Child £3 (ages 4-16), Family £13
- Season tickets: Adults £15, Child £12, Family £40 - Season tickets are valid for one year and also allow entry to Castell Henllys Iron Age Village (which is 47 min/ 30 miles away).
- Free guided tours daily - subject to availability
- Open: Winter hours 10am - 3pm / Rest of the year, 10am - 5pm
- Parking: Free car park
- Address: Carew, Tenby, Pembrokeshire, SA70 8SL
- Website: carewcastle.com

How to get there:

- Car: M4 from Cardiff to A48 to A477 in St Clears. Follow A477 to Carew
- Estimated travel time: 1 hour 50 minutes
- Train: Nearest train stations are Pembroke

Dock and Tenby. I think Tenby is the easiest station, but if you plan to stay in Pembroke, you can do so from Pembroke Dock. Depart from Cardiff Central to Fishguard (2h 21 min/ 18 stops), exit Carmarthen then walk south-west to Station Approach, take the train from Cararthen to Pembroke Dock, exit Pembroke Dock and walk out of entrance north, Adj 25 & 2 Water Street - Railway Street then take bus 360/Tenby, exit War Memorial, walk about 2 minuts to destination

- Estimated travel time: 3 hours 30 minutes

- Bus: 360/Pembroke Dock - exit War Memorial, walk about 2 minutes north on A4075 to destination

- Estimated travel time: 35 minutes

Services

- Dogs allowed

- Cafe

- No drones

- Gift Shop

- Toilets

Nearby: Tenby (12 min/ 6.7 miles), Manorbier Castle (14 miles/ 5.8 miles), Presipe Beach (Manorbier), Coastal Path (Manorbier), Castell Henllys Iron Age Village (47 min/ 30 miles away)

I highly recommend Carew Castle

Carmarthen Castle

If you are in the area and enjoy outdoor markets (on Wednesdays and Saturdays), then give the castle a look-over and then enjoy a stroll and shop. This castle dates back to the 1100's and was first built out of wood and was destroyed then rebuilt in stone - which was destroyed many times over. The castle has an interesting history, but today's ruins are not intriguing.

- Cost: Free
- Parking: Street/pay and display
- Address: Carmarthen, SA31 1AD

How to get there:

- Car: M4 then at roundabout take 2nd exit onto A48, next roundabout take 3rd exit, stay on A48, travel 11 mi. At roundabout take 2nd exit onto A40, then take 3rd exit onto A4242. At next roundabout take the 1st exit onto Morfa Ln/B4312, then at next roundabout take 2nd exit to destination
- Estimated travel time: 1 hour 20 minutes
- Train: Cardiff Central to Milford Haven - Transport for Wales (2h/ 14 stops), exit Carmarthen and walk about 7 minutes - Station

Approach rd, left over bridge, then take a right on Castle Hill, take a right on Church St, left on Queen St, left on King St to destination

· Estimated travel time: 2 hours 9 minutes

Services

· Dogs allowed

· No drones

Nearby: National Botanic Gardens (12 min/ 9.4 miles away), Laugharne Castle (17 min/ 13 miles away), Kidwelly Castle (18 min/ 9.4 miles away)

Castell Coch

I absolutely love this romantic castle; the first sighting is just as intoxicating as the tenth. This 19th-century Gothic Revival castle's interior was inspired by Aesop, the fairytale themed rooms will have you marvel at the whimsical features throughout the compact circular castle; Lady Bute's bedroom will leave the ladies who visit wishing for one nights stay in the magical room - intricately decorated with mischievous monkeys and butterflies painted upon the ceiling tiles above her 6-post crystal-ball bed.

Each time I visit Lady Bute's bedroom I spend a lengthy amount of time taking in the details and it never fails that newcomers that enter the room rarely do - they are in and out within a couple of minutes. I want to yell out to them - "you missed the dragon sink faucet" and "did you notice that each monkey is different?" Of course they didn't notice, most are in too much of a hurry to get to the next sight. Please do not be like them - take the time to notice the details, you'll be happy that you did.

While not large in size, Castle Coch packs a punch of perfection inside and out, yet if you're watching your spending and you've been inside Cardiff Castle, you might want to save your money and enjoy this fairytale castle from the outside - with that said, I've been inside this castle three times and I easily spend about twenty minutes in Lady Bute's bedroom, as I mentioned above, it is phenomenal.

Getting married? It is a splendid location for your nuptuals.

If you are fans of the TV show Merlin, you will recognize it - along with other shows it has been featured in, such as: *Dr. Who*, *The Worst Witch* and *Tracy Beaker.*

To complete your day, meander the woodlands and discover animal and fairytale wood carvings. The trails are marked and range from 45-minutes to an hour and half. Other than the extremely steep hill that leads up to the castle - Castell Coch and it's woodlands, Fforest Fawr, is my favorite place to visit in the Cardiff area.

- Cadw - Yes
- Cost: Adults £7.70, Juniors (5-17) £4.60, Family Tickets (2 adults/3 children) £21.60, Seniors £6.10
- A handheld device is provided for an audio tour
- Parking: Free
- Open: 9:30am - 5pm - except July & August, 9:30am - 6pm

November & December, 10am - 4pm

- Address: Cardiff, CF15 7JS
- Website: cadw.gov.wales

How to get there:

- Car: Take A470 to Merthyr Rd/A4054, exit for A4054/B4262 from A470. Continue on Merthyr Rd/A4054 to destination.
- Estimated Travel Time: 30 minutes
- Bus: Bus lines 23/26 gold - The 23 bus Rhiwbina via Pantmawr (18 minutes with 12 stops), exit Merthyr Road Shops, the take G1 Gwaelod-y-garth (12 minutes/ 9 stops) - exit Bute Street then walk 15 minutes to the castle.
- Alternative route: Bus line 26 gold Blackwood, ride (27 minutes/ 16 stops), exit at Car-

diff Rd/Llys Hafn then walk 33 minutes to the castle.

- Estimated Travel Time: 1 hour

- Bike: You can follow the National Cycle Rte 8, Taff Trail - follow the river heading north. Turn right onto Iron Bridge Rd/National Cycle Rte 8, turn left to stay on Iron Bridge Rd/Rte 8, then turn left onto Merthyr Rd/National Cycle Rte 8, turn right onto Mill Rd and continue onto Castle Rd - your destination will be on the left. There are not any bike racks at the bottom of the hill, but there is at the trail head near the castle.

- Uber: From downtown Cardiff, £12 - £15

Services

- Dogs no allowed - with exception to guide dogs

- No drone

- Cafe

- Gift shop

- Toilets

Nearby: Fforest Fawr (0 min/0miles away), National Roman Legion (27 minutes/ 19 miles away), Dewstow Gardens and Grotto (35 min/ 27 miles away)

I highly recommend Castell Coch

Chepstow Castle

This castle is a real treat to discover and is massive. Built around 1067 and continued through 1690, the castle's mass grew above the cliffs of the Wye River as each new owner added to the structure. Chepstow has the oldest wooden doors in all of Europe - 800 years old and are on display. Expect to be here for a few hours, perhaps pack a picnic and enjoy the scenery.

- Cadw: Yes
- Cost: Adults £7.70, Kids (5-17) £4.60, Family (2 adults/3 kids) £21.60, Seniors £6.10
- Parking: pay and display parking
- Open: 9:30am - 5pm
- Address: 1 Bridge Street, Chepstow, NP16 5EY
- Website: cadw.gov.wales

How to get there:

- Car: M4 - take the M4 and M48 to Wye Valley Link Rd/A466 in Monmouthshire. Take exit 2 then follow Wye Valley Link Rd/A466 and A48 to Nelson Street in Chepstow
- Estimated travel time: 39 minutes
- Train and Bus: Cardiff Central to Newport,

walk about 8 minutes to the bus - Newport Friars Walk (stand 7) bus line 73 Chepstow, then walk about 6 minutes to castle

- Estimated travel time: 1 hour 30 minutes

- Bus: National Express, Sophia Gardens, Cardiff to Chepstow (£6.60/ 50 min), walk to destination

- Estimated travel time: 1 hour

- Uber: From downtown Cardiff, £42 - £55+

Services

- Dogs allowed - ground floors only
- No drones
- Gift shop
- Toilets

Nearby: Tintern Abbey (12 mins/ 5.4 miles), head to Raglan Castle (28 mins/ 15 miles), Usk Castle (10 mins/ 7.8 miles)

I highly recommend Chepstow Castle

Cilgerran Castle

High above the River Teifi, this castle with it's imposing towers is on my to visit list. Sorry that I am not able to comment at this time; I do suggest you check out the website to see if it should be added to your itinerary.

Cadw: Yes

- Cost: Adult £4.50, Juniors (5-17) £2.60, Family £12.50, Senior £3.60
- Open: 10am - 5pm, April 2 - November 3; 10am - 4pm, Nov 4 - March 31, exception - closed December 24, 25, 26 and January 1
- Parking: Street parking
- Address: Cardigan, SA43 2SF
- Website: cadw.gov.wales

How to get there:

- Car: M4, continue on A48 towards Pembrokeshire, then A40 to B4298. When you get to B4332 to A478. Turn left on High Street and right on Castle Square
- Estimated travel time: 2 hours
- Train: Cardiff Central to Milford Haven (2h 20min/ 17 stops), exit Clunderwen- walk about a minute to War Memorial, take bus 430/Cardigan (45 min/ 20 stops), exit Cardiff Arms, wallk 2 minutes - north-west on High Street towards Castle Square, keep to the right to destination
- Estimated travel time: 3 hours 30 minutes
- Bus: Cardigan, route no 142, Haverfordwest-Cardigan

Services

- Dogs allowed - ground floors only
- No drones
- Cafe
- Gift Shop
- Toilets

Nearby: Cardigan Castle (8 min/ 3.4 miles away), Castell Henllys Iron Age Village (16 min/ 8.5 miles away), Coastal Paths, Fishguard (31 min/ 19 miles away), St Davids Bishop's Palace (56 min/ 35 miles away),

Coity Castle

If you are like me and want to put a check mark next to all the accessible castles in Wales, then add Coity to a days adventuring. But if you are limited in time, then you're not missing anything special - instead, check out one of the numerous castles in Wales that are worth seeing.

- Cost: Free
- Open: 10am - 6pm
- Parking: Free
- Address: Coity, Bridgend, CF35 6BG
- Website: cadw.gov.wales

How to get there:

- Car: M4 to A4061 in Bridgend County Borough. Take exit 36, follow A4061 and W Plas Rd to destination

- Estimated travel time: 35 minutes

- Train: Cardiff Central toward Swansea (16 min/non-stop), exit Pen-y-Bont/ Bridgend, walk about 7 minutes to Bus Station, take bus 76 Bettws (4 min/5 stops), exit Litchard Cross, walk about 20 minutes to destination

- Estimated travel time: 55 minutes

- Bus: Cardiff bus 201 towards Swansea, exit Sarn Odeon and walk about 4 minutes to Sarn Sainsbury take bus 16 towards Bridgend, exit Lithard Cross and walk 19 minutes to the castle

- Estimated travel time: 1 hour 30 minutes

Services

- Dogs allowed

- No drones

- No services

Nearby: Ewenny Priory (2.39 miles away), Ogmore Castle (3.78 miles away), The Royal Mint (21 min/ 14 miles away), Castell Coch (26 min/18 miles away), Caerphilly Castle (32 min/ 22 miles away)

Cyfarthfa Castle Museum - see Museums

Dinefwr Castle

Located on top of a hill, near Newton House, you need to traipse through sheep pastures and woodland to reach it. As far as castles go, it's just like so many other ruins - but it's surroundings, Dinefwr Park, make it worth visiting. The 800 acre park has wide open grassy hillsides, wildlife (birds, sheep, deer, cattle), bog woods with a boardwalk and dense woodland.

When you come to the sign post that arrows to the trail head, park your car - there is a spot right there in front of the sign post in the middle of the road (at the Y) - your car will fit fine without blocking driveways. If you keep driving you will come to Newton House and they charge for you to park. The other alternative for free parking is to park inside the property main gate, or just outside the gate, and walk in; it is a pretty long walk from the entrance gate to the sights.

If you plan on going inside Newton House, visit it first before walking up to the castle - otherwise your shoes may be very muddy, which will not make them happy.

*Newton House information - see Gardens & Heritage Homes

- Cost: Free
- Open: 10am - 4pm daily, with exception -

December 24, 25 & 26 and January 1

- Parking: Parking lot charges - £8.50 per adult - yikes! It includes entrance into Newton house. If you are *not* interested in the house, do not drive all the way down the driveway - park outside gate for free and walk through the pasture to the castle - or park where I explained above.
- Address: Llandeilo, SA19 6RT
- Website: cadw.gov.wales

How to get there:

- Car: M4 then continue onto A483
- Estimated travel time: 1 hour 30 minutes

Services

- No drones
- No toilets at site, but are available at Newton House located on property

Nearby: Newton House (on property), Carreg Cennen (3.84 miles away), Aberglasney Gardens,

Dryslwyn Castle (3.68 miles away), Paxton's Tower (7 miles away)

• These sights make a perfect day trip. Start at Paxtons Tower then visit Dryslwyn - Aberglasney Gardens is between Dryslwyn and Dinefwr Castle, just follow the sign to the gardens - located only a minute or two from turn off - and then after Dinefwr head over to Carreg Cennen.

Dryslwyn Castle

I really enjoyed this ruin, even though there is not much left to it. The view is amazing and the day we went was right after the valley experienced flooding, which really gave us a clear perspective of the overflow.

Dryslwyn Castle is a nice place to hike for a picnic. There is a car park directly across the road and stairs part way up the hill. It's an easy walk up, but if it has been raining, expect the grassy hillside to be slippery.

- Cost: Free
- Parking: Free public car park
- Address: B4297, Carmarthen, SA32 8JQ
- Website: cadw.gov.uk

How to get there:

- Car: M4 then continue onto A470, then B4297, take 2nd exit onto A48, next roundabout take 4th exit onto Llandeilo Rd/A76, left on B4297, slide left onto B4300, right onto B4297 to destination

- Estimated travel time: 1 hour 21 minutes

Services

- Dogs allowed
- No drones
- No services

Nearby: Paxton's Tower (8 min/ 3.5 miles away), Aberglasney Gardens (5 min/ 3 miles away), Dinefwr Castle & Newton House (14 min/ 6.9 miles away), Carreg Cennen Castle (19 min/ 9.3 miles away)

Grosmont Castle

Along with Skenfrith and White - Grosmont Castle was built by Normans as part of their stronghold over the area. What remains is a little more interesting to see than the other two, but with that said, it will only take a few minutes to take in what remains.

- Cost: Free
- Open: 10am - 4pm
- Parking: on street, then walk across what seems like private property to the castle

bridge

- Address: Grosmont, Abergavanny, NP7 8EP

- Website: cadw.gov.uk

How to get there:

- Car: M4/Newport - junction 26, take the A4051 exit to Newport, then take 1st exit at roundabout onto Malpas Rd/A4051, after 1.5 miles, at roundabout take the 3rd exit onto A4042, keep on A4042 exiting onto A4042 at each roundabout (Turnpike Rd, Croesyceiliog Bypass and Usk Rd are all A4042). When you get to Hardwick Gyratory/A40 exit roundabout, 4th exit, then road slights left onto A465. You will be on A465 for 11 miles then turn right onto B4347 follow road to destination

- Estimated travel time: 1 hour

Services

- Dogs allowed

- No drones

- No services

Nearby: Skenfrith Castle (11 min/ 5 miles away), White Castle (17 min/ 7.3 miles away), Raglan Castle (31 min/ 21 miles away)

Kidwelly Castle

One of the best preserved castles and in my top five favorites, Kidwelly is worth the hour drive from Cardiff - try to go in the morning before it gets busy. What makes this castle different from others is that each of the four towers are shaped differently. This castle is very well preserved, in fact, you can walk along the outer wall for a fantastic view of the village.

Those of you interested in ghost stories - tales of a headless ghost that roams the countryside around Kidwelly inspired the story *"The Headless Horseman"*.

- Cadw: Yes
- Cost: Adults £6.00, Children £3.70, Family £17.10, Seniors £4.80
- Parking: Free
- Open: 9:30am - 4pm, 5pm or 6pm - closing time depends on season
- Address: Castle Rd, Kidwelly, SA17 5BQ
- Website: cadw.gov.wales

How to get there:

- Car: M4 - Follow M4 to Pontarddulais Rd/A4138 in Hendy, take exit 48, continue along at roundabout take 2nd exit, A4138, at roundabout take 3rd exit continue onto Llethri Rd, left onto Millfield Rd/A476 roundabout

Stradey Rd/B4308, sharp right onto Old Rd to destination

- Estimated Travel Time: 1 hour 25 minutes
- Train: Cardiff Central to Fishguard Harbour (1h 30mins/ 8 stops) exit Kidwelly and walk about 13 minutes to castle
- Estimated Travel Time: 1 hour 43 minutes
- Bus: National Express, Cardiff Coach Station, Sofia Gardens to Llanelli (£13.20/ Direct 2 hours) then Llaneilli Bus Station to Kidwelly X11
- Estimated Travel Time: 2 hour 30 minutes

Services

- Dogs allowed - ground floor only
- No drones
- Cafe
- Gift shop
- Toilets

Nearby: Aberglasney Gardens (32 min/ 21 miles away), Paxton's Tower (28 min/ 17 miles away), Dryslwyn Castle (30 min/ 20 miles away), Oystermouth Castle (45 min/ 23 miles away), Swansea Museum (42 min/ 21 miles away)

I highly recommend Kidwelly Castle

Laugharne Castle

One of many erected as part of the chain of Norman coastal castles from Chepstow to Pembroke.

The town offers plenty of activities to enjoy: pubs, shops and hiking paths. Poet Dylan Thomas lived and wrote in his boathouse and writing shed located just beyond the castle's shadow.

This castle is a 90-minute drive from Cardiff and not worth the drive by itself, but when paired with Oystermouth and Swansea Museum or time spent on the beach - it is worth a visit. The Mumbles is a beautiful area to spend a day or longer.

- Cadw: Yes
- Cost: Adult £4.50, Juniors £2.60, Family £12.50, Seniors £3.60
- Parking: Free parking below castle
- Open: The castle is not open year-round, but makes a fantastic view while having a picnic in the park
- Address: King St, Laugharne, Carmarthen, SA33 4SF
- Website: cadw.gov.wales

How to get there:

- Car: M4 - continue to A40 to A4066 in

Laugharne

- Estimated travel time: 1 hour 30 minutes

- Train: Cardiff Central to Carmarthen (2 hrs 22 min/ 10 stops), in Carmarthen change onto Milford Haven (16 min/ non-stop), exit Whitland and walk about 1 minute to Railway Station bus line 381/ Tenby (2 min/ 2 stops) exit Pen-y-Back bus line 222 Pendine (20 stops), exit Brown's Hotel - walk about 2 minutes to castle

- Estimated travel time: 3 hour 35 minutes

- Bus: National Express, Cardiff Coach Station, Sofia Gardens to Llanelli (£13.20/ 1 hr 50 mins) Llanelli Bus Station to Laugharne towards Pendine bus 222

- Estimated travel time: 3 hours

Services

- Dogs allowed on ground floors
- No drones
- Cafe
- Gift Shop

Nearby: Dylan Thomas Boathouse (below castle at shore, follow paved path), Dryslwyn Castle (32 min/ 24 miles away), Aberglasney Gardens (33 min/ 24.8 miles away) Dinefwr Castle & Newton House (41 min/ 27 miles away), Lamphey Bishop's

Palace (35 min/ 25 miles away)

Llansteffan Castle

Stellar views overlooking the Carmarthen Bay is what the castle has going for it. It looks to be a great place to have a picnic and relax looking at the view. You might want to include it in your day castle hopping, but it won't be the end of the world if you don't. Nearby Kidwelly is sure to be a much better choice - I have not been to this site yet.

- Cost: Free
- Open: 10am - 4pm - Closed December 24, 25, 26 and January 1
- Parking: Car park near castle, about 800 meters away
- Address: Llansteffan, Carmarthen, SA33 5LW
- Website: llansteffancastle.com and cadw.gov.wales

How to get there:

- Car: M4 to A48, taking 2nd exit at roundabout, stay on A48 until you come to B4312 exit towards Johnstown/Llansteffan, then turn right onto Llansteffan Rd/B4312, left on Church Rd follow road to the right and to your destination

- Estimated travel time: 1 hour 30 minutes

Services

- Dogs allowed
- No drones
- No services

Nearby: Kidwelly Castle (4 miles away), Laugharne Castle and Poet Dylan Thomas Writing Shed (3 miles away)

Manorbier Castle

It was an unusually warm and dry January, so we decided to check out the coastal paths and beaches in the area - that's when we came across Manorbier Castle. Unfortunately, it was closed for winter renovations. I'll make a trip back later on, because it does look interesting enough to check out. The castle is perched above the beach, it is nicely preserved, has a lovely garden within the walls and movie makers have used it - you can see it in the flick: "The Lion, The Witch and The Wardrobe."

- Cadw: No
- Cost: Adults £5.50, Seniors £4, Children £3 and Family ticket £15
- Open: Normally open 10am - 5pm every day. Closed during private functions, visit website

for dates closed.

- Parking: Car park at Manorbier Beach or pay and display at the beach - which is free during winter.

- Address: Manorbier, Tenby, SA70 7SY

- Website:manorbiercastle.co.uk

How to get there:

- Car: M4, then take A48 to A40 and continue to on until A477 and then take roundabout 1st exit B4318, turn right, continue onto Coal Lane, turn left onto The Ridgeway, turn right, then left onto A4139, turn right onto B4585, turn right to destination

- Estimated travel time: 1 hour 50 minutes

- Train: Cardiff Central/Milford Haven (3h/ 24 stops), exit Johnston (Pembs), walk about 2 minutes south on Station Road to Railway Hotel, take bus 349/Tenby (1h 5min/ 32 stops), exit Manorbier House, walk about 2 minutes to destination - east turn right onto B4585 keeping to the left to destination

- Estimated travel time: 5 hours

- Bus: National Express, Sophia Gardens, Cardiff to Tenby (under £20/ 3h or 4h), then take bus 349/Withybush (20 min/ 13 stops), exit Manorbier House, walk about 2 minutes to destination - east turn right onto B4585 keeping to the left to destination

- Estimated travel time: 3 hour 20 minutes/ 4 hour 20 minutes

Services

- Dogs allowed
- No drones
- Cafe
- Gift Shop
- Toilets

Nearby: Coastal walk, Presipe Beach (1.5 mile away - coastal path), Skrinkle Haven Beach (5 min/ 1.5 miles away - by street) Lamphey Bishop's Palace (12 min/ 4.3 miles away), Tenby (5.9 miles away), Saundersfoot (8.5 miles away), Laugharne Castle and Dylan Thomas' Boathouse (41 min/ 25 miles away)

Neath Castle

There's not much left of this castle - just the twin tower gatehouse. If you are in Neath, then maybe do a drive-by on your way to Neath Abbey.

- Cost: Free
- Parking: Street parking
- Address: 1 Castle View, Neath, SA11 3LW

How to get there:

- Car: M4 to exit 43, A465 - take A474 at roundabout take 1st exit Prince of Wales Dr/B4434 to Castle View, turn left onto High St and then right onto Old Market St, which becomes Castle St

- Estimated travel time: 1 hour

- Train: Cardiff Central, the train leaves every 30 minutes (37 min/ 3 stops), exit Castell-Nedd/Neath. Walk about 6 minutes to castle

- Estimated travel time: 43 minutes

- Bus: Cardiff Coach Station, Sophia Gardens, National Express to Neath, it is direct (£6.90)

- Estimated travel time: 55 minutes

Services

- Dog friendly

- No drones

Nearby: Combine with Aberdulais Falls (2.2 miles), Neath Abbey (1.5 miles) and Neath Abbey Ironworks (1.6 miles). It's a 7 minute drive northeast to the falls and a 7 minute drive to the abbey and ironworks, going the opposite directions from the castle.

Old Beaupre' Castle

The wealthy and influentual Bassett family showed off their status and fashion sense by adding a Renaissance porch to Old Beaupre'. It is an unusual castle enhancement and worth seeing.

To get to this castle you need to park at the foot gate entrance and walk through a farmers fields and cross over a couple of foot gates to get to the structure. Dress appropriately for maneuvering around sheep droppings, mud and climbing foot gates. It takes less than ten minutes to walk to the ruin and is worth the effort. If you have difficulty walking distances and would like to see Old Beaupre', there is a driveway that goes straight to the property; it belongs to the homeowner who lives behind the castle - I am unsure if he welcomes the use of his driveway. Please pay attention and obey any posted signs.

- Cost: Free
- Parking: Free on street
- Address: Cowbridge, CF71 7LT
- Website: cadw.gov.wales

How to get there:

- Car: M4 toward Cardiff Airport, exit roundabout onto A4232, use left lane, take A48/A4050 ramp to Cardiff West/Barry, follow A48 signs, roundabout 2nd exit onto A48, stay on for 6 miles

- Estimated travel time: 25 minutes

Services

- Dogs not allowed
- No drones
- No toilets

Nearby: Tinkinswood Burial Chamber (15 min/ 8.40 miles), St. Lythan's Burial Chamber (17 min/ 9.18 miles) and Dyffryn Gardens (16 min/ 9 miles) - all these sites are within minutes from each other

I recommend this castle due to the unusual Renaissance porch

Ogmore Castle

Ogmore Castle, is located near Ogmore-By-Sea; we just happened upon it on our first day trip venturing Wales. We were driving to Dunraven Bay when we came upon it and while there is little left of this ruin, I was thrilled out of my mind.

Don't end your tour of the area at the castle. Cross the river via stepping stones and follow the walking path through the gate. The trail takes you to the medieval village of Merthyr Mawr. This small community offers a few houses, church and cemetery. If you have never seen a thatched roof, you will here.

For those of you interested in ghost stories, the "white lady" is said to roam the ruins.

- Cost: Free
- Parking: free
- Address: Ogmore, Bridgend, CF32 0QP
- Website: cadw.gov.wales

How to get there:

- Car: M4, exit A473 then at roundabout take the 1st exit, staying on A473, you will encounter a couple more roundabouts, stay on A473, Waterton Rd and then Bypass Rd/ A48. Keep on A48 to roundabout to Ewenny Rd/B4265 continue to Ogmore Rd, turn right, stay on Ogmore Rd to destination

- Estimated travel time: 32 minutes

- Train: Cardiff Central to Swansea GWR (18 min/ 1 stop), exit Pen-y-Bont/Bridgend, you then need to walk to Station Hill, about 2 minutes, then wait up to 13 minutes for bus 303/Barry. Ride bus 303/Barry (8 min/ 8 stops), exit Pelican Inn, walk about three minutes to destination

- Estimated travel time: 1 hour

- Bus: Central Station JM T9 TrawsCymru (33 min/ 7 stops), exit at Airport, walk to bus 303/Bridgend (1h 12 min/ 51 stops), exit Pelican Inn then walk to destination

- Estimated travel time: 2 hours

Services

- Dog allowed

- No drones

- Toilets

- Horseback riding available at farm next to the castle

Nearby: Medieval village Merthyr Mawr (walk over stepping stones and follow path to village - about a 15 minute walk - or 8 min/ 3.1 mile care ride), Dunraven at Southerndown (10 min/ 3.9 miles away), The Royal Mint (29 min/ 16 miles away)

Oystermouth Castle

This is not a large castle, but it's an enjoyable maze of rooms. To access the glass suspension floor in the Sacristy, you have to enter through the gift stop. Since this is where you need to return the laminated map, your proof of entry, I suggest you enter the Sacristy last.

You might want to plan to visit Oystermouth Castle and Swansea Museum on the same day. If you are not pressed for time, consider riding bikes - you can rent them in The Mumbles; park at the castle then cycle back along the bay front to Swansea. It will take about 45 minutes each way on bike. On the way back to The Mumbles be sure to stop at the parlor that is located along the path for a scoop of ice cream - go ahead, you deserve it.

- Cost: Adults £4, Children under 5 Free, Family Ticket £11

- Parking: Free parking on the grass next to castle or pay and display below castle

- Open: 11am - 5pm, April 1 - September 30, October weekends only - closed winter months

- Address: Castle Ave, The Mumbles, Swansea, SA3 4BA

- Website: swansea.gov.uk

How to get there:

- Car: M4 to Junction 42, take the A483, merge onto Fabian Way/A483 then at the roundabout take the 1st exit onto The Mumbles Rd/A4067, then at the next roundabout take the 2nd exit onto Newton Rd/B4593, turn right onto Castle Ave to destination

- Estimated travel time: 1 hour

- Train: Cardiff Central to Milford Haven, Transport for Wales (1h 4min/ 8 stops), exit Swansea then walk 1 minute to High Street Station and wait for UniBus 10/Singleton (20 min/ 12 stops), exit Hospital, then take 2A/

Limeslade (14 min/ 12 stops), exit Newton Rd
and then walk about a minute to destination

- Estimated travel time: 2 hours
- Bus: National Express, Sophia Gardens, Cardiff to Swansea (£6.90/ 1hr 15 min), Bus station (Stand W) bus 2A/Caswell Bay (26 min/
20 stops), exit Newton Rd, walk one minute
to destination

Services

- Dogs allowed
- No drones
- Cafe
- Gift shop
- Toilets

Nearby: Swansea Museum (10 min/ 4.6 miles),
Coastal Path

I recommend visiting Oystermouth Castle

Oxwich Castle

This is another castle that you do not need to
bother with, unless you want to see every castle in
Wales. In my opinion it's not worth the fee - taking
only minutes to wander around the interior.

- Cadw: Yes

- Cost: Adults £4.50, Children (5-17) £2.60, Family £12.50, Seniors £3.60

- Open: 10am - 5pm, Wednesday - Sunday - closed November 4 - March 31

- Parking: Car park on grass - Free

- Address: Oxwich Castle, Oxwich, SA3 1ND

- Website: cadw.gov.wales

How to get there:

- Car: M4 to A483 - take exit 42, from M4, and continue on Fabian Way/A483 to your destination

- Estimated travel time: 1 hour 17 minutes

- Train then Bus: Cardiff Central to Swansea (35 min/ 2 stops) exit Port Talbot Parkway, walk 2 minutes to stand 6, take X3 Swansea (33 min/ 21 stops) exit Bus Station stand G and go to stand S (about 1 min) get on bus line 118 Rhossili (21 mins/ 16 stops) exit Railway Inn and get on bus line 117 Oxwich Green (25 mins/ 15 stops) exit Greenways Leisure Park walk about 3 minutes to the castle

- Estimated travel time: 3 hours

- Bus: Cardiff to Swansea - bus line 201 (1h 15 min/ 3 stops) from Swansea Bus Station walk to Stand S 118 Rhossili (41 min/ 29 stops) exit Perriswood Turn and walk about 1 minute to Oxwich Towers take bus line 117

Parkmill and exit Greenways Leisure Park (4 mins/ 2 stops), walk about 3 minutes to Oxwich Castle

- Estimated travel time: 3 hours

Services

- Dogs allowed
- No drones
- Cafe
- Gift shop
- Toilets

Nearby: Oxwich Beach, The Mumbles (24 min/ 11 miles away), Weobley Castle (18 min/ 7.2 miles away), Swansea Museum (27 min/ 13 miles away)

Pembroke Castle

Birthplace of Henry VII, Pembroke Castle is packed with education and fun for the whole family. There are so many rooms filled with timeline facts, that I soon found my brain overloaded and decided to enjoy a cup of goodness and a cake as I waited for my boyfriend to do the same. The guy loves all that tedious information, yet he too found himself overwhelmed halfway through all that is offered. Together we found more pleasure sipping cappuccino's while watching faux knights teach kids and adults how to be knightsman.

Did Pembroke Castle make a good impact on me? Not really. In all fairness, it is a nicely preserved castle that has a total "wow" factor on the outside - yet, it fell short of impressing me. I have revisited a number of castles and I can honestly say, if I was given a free ticket, I wouldn't return to Pembroke. If you are wondering which castles I have been inside more than once, they are: Cardiff (2x) and Castle Coch (3x) - and I would be happy to revisit Raglan and Conwy (North Wales).

- Cadw: No

- Cost: Adults £7, Child £6, Seniors £6

- Free Guided Tours: ask for given times

- Open: 10am - 5pm - closed major holidays, check website

- Parking: Car park, pay and display

- Address: Pembroke, SA71 4LA

- Website: pembrokecastle.co.uk

How to get there:

- Car: M4 to Junction 49, then take the A48/Carmarthen exit. In Carmarthen, take 2nd exit at roundabout onto A40 towards St Clears, then at the next roundabout take the 1st exit, keeping on A40/St Clears. Then in St Clears take the 1st exit onto the A477/Tenby, follow the signs to Pembroke Dock. Turn left onto A4075 for Pembroke, then take 2nd exit at roundabout onto A4139 to castle.

- Estimated travel time: 1 hour 50 minutes

- Train: Cardiff Central to Swansea GWR (54 min/ 4 stops), then take Transport for Wales train to Pembroke Dock (2h/ 13 stops) exit Pembroke, walk 14 minutes to castle

- Estimated travel time: 3 hour 38 minutes

- Bus: National Express - Sophia Gardens, Cardiff to Pembroke (£19.20 or £16.10 - depending on length of ride), walk to castle

- Estimated travel time: 3 hours or 4 hours

Services

- Dogs allowed during the day, not at after-hour events

- No drones

- Cafe

- Gift Shop

- Toilets

Nearby: Lamphey Bishop's Palace (5 min/ 2 miles away), Carew Castle & Tidal Mill (7min/ 4.2 miles away), Manorbier Castle (15 min/ 6.3 miles away), Coastal Walk, Folly Farm Adventure Park (16min/ 11 miles away)

Raglan Castle

My favorite castle in South Wales is Raglan. This castle was built to impress and everything about it says "wow." With it's intricate wood carvings and massive windows, it doesn't take much imagination to comprehend how amazing the interior of this castle was.

Raglan Castle has an appealing past that includes many stories, even a dark one. Working up the social ladder, William Herbert went from Squire to Baron of Raglan and eventually became the guardian of Henry Tudor, whom later became King Henry VII. Young Henry had to live in hiding at Raglan as a child for his own personal safety.

One of the more interesting tales is the day William Herbert invited twenty-five prestigious neighboring men to a feast of celebration, which was actually his ploy to murder them all. It was a jolly good time around the dining table, that is until the end of the meal - when each guest met his fate with a glass of poisonous wine.

This castle not only has an interesting history, but visitors can see innovated props of the height of technology during medieval times. And for the fans of the TV show *Merlin*, episode - *"Le Morte d'Arthur"* - was filmed here.

The chapter photo is this castle.

- Cadw: Yes

- Cost: Adults £7.70, Kids (5-17) £4.60, Family £21.60, Seniors £6.10

- Parking: Free on grass surface

- Open: 9:30am - 5pm, Except during winter: 10am - 4pm

- Address: Castle Rd, Raglan, NP15 2BT

- Website: cadw.gov.wales

How to get there:

- Car: M4 East towards Newport, Junction 24 exit and take A449 exit to The Midlands/ Monmouth, keep left at the fork, follow signs staying on A449, take exit ramp A40 to Abergavenny, at roundabout take the 5th exit to stay on A40 then turn on Castle Rd to destination

- Estimated travel time: 40 minutes

- Train: Cardiff Central GWR - London Paddington to Newport (12 min/ 1 stop), walk about 7 minutes to Newport Friars Walk bus station (Stand 7), take bus 60/Monmouth (39 min/ 43 stops), exit St Cadoc's Church, walk 13 minutes to destination

- Estimated travel time: 1 hour 17 minutes

- Bus: National Express, Sophia Gardens, Cardiff to Newport (£3.60/ 30 min)- Newport Friars Walk bus station (Stand 7), take bus 60/ Monmouth (39 min/ 43 stops), exit St Cadoc's

Church, walk 13 minutes to destination

- Estimated travel time: 1 hour 15 minutes

Services

- Dogs allowed on ground floor level
- No drone
- Cafe
- Water refill station available
- Gift Shop
- Toilets

Nearby: Chepstow (28 min/ 15 miles away), Tintern Abbey (25 min/ 12 miles away), Goodrich (20 min/ 15 miles away *in England* - highly recommended), White (20 min/ 9 miles away), Skenfrith Castles (27 min/ 17 miles away) and Grosmont (29 min/ 20 miles away)

- We did the above itinerary and even though it made a long day, we had plenty of time to visit every sight and make it back to Cardiff before nightfall. We spent about 2 hours at each major attraction, except the last three castles only require a few minutes.

I highly recommend Raglan Castle

Skenfrith Castle

One of three castles that controlled the area between the River Wye and the Black Mountains. The trio (Grosmont, Skenfrith and White) were founded by Norman Lord William Fitz Osbern in the early 12th century. Today the outer walls and Keep are the only buildings intact.

- Cost: Free
- Open: Year-round, 10am - 4pm
- Parking: Car Park
- Address: Skenfrith, Abergavenny, NP7 8UH
- Website: cadw.gov.wales

How to get there:

- Car: M4, A449 and A40 to Cinderhill St/B4233 in Monmouth. Take exit towards Monmouth/Trefynwy/Trellech/B4293 - you will stay on B4293 and B4347 to destination
- Estimated travel time: 1 hour

Services

- Dogs allowed
- No drones
- No toilets

Nearby: Ragland Castle (11.5 miles) Grosmont Castle (4.12 miles away), White Castle (5.26 miles away), Llanthony Priory (10.7 miles) *the distance is short, but these are country roads - expect to double your travel time.

Tretower Court and Castle

Once a dignified residence for lords and ladies, it was abandoned shortly after 1700 and is now a Cadw property. According to the Cadw website, the Medieval kitchen, buttery, pantry and the great hall have been restored to their 1460 grandeur. All furniture is 15th-century replicas.

Named after it's massive circular tower, Tretower Castle was built to proclaim the Picard family climb up the social ladder. If a visit to Tretower Castle for the tower is not enough of a reason - then perhaps the restored court and 15th century garden will make it worth your trip. I have not been to the court or castle, so I really cannot say.

The court and castle are available for venue hire.

- Cadw: Yes
- Cost: Adult £7.70, Juniors £4.60 (5 - 17), Family (2 parents/3 kids) £21.60, Seniors £6.10
- Open: 10am - 5pm daily, April 1 - Nov 3 & 10am - 4pm Nov 4 - March 31 - closed December 24, 25, 26 and January 1 - check website for unexpected closures
- Parking: Car park and roadside parking - Free

- Address: Tretower, Crickhowell, NP8 1RD
- Website: cadw.gov.wales

How to get there:

- Car: M4 (E) to Newport, Junction 26, take A4051 to Newport, at roundabout take 1st exit onto Malpas Rd/A4051, then at roundabout exit onto A4042, keep on A4042 through roundabouts towards Usk, then exit to Heads of the Valleys Rd/A465, use any ramp, at roundabout, take 3rd exit onto Abergavenny Rd/A4077. Keep on A4077, turning right onto Crickhowell Rd/A4077 then left, staying on A4077, then turn right onto Crickhowell Bridge/New Rd/A4077, turn left onto A40 for 3 miles to destination.

- Estimated travel time: 1 hour

- Train: Cardiff Central to Manchester Piccadilly (37 min/ 3 stops), exit Abergavenny, walk about 3 minutes to Station Road bus stop, take the X43 TrawsCymru bus (21 min/ 13 stops), exit Gilfaes Turn and then walk about 10 minutes to destination - take care walking along A40 and road to destination.

- Estimated travel time: 1 hour 25 minutes

- Bus: Greyfriars Road GH in Cardiff (direct bus) to Abergavenny. In Abergavenny take the X43 TrawsCymru bus (21 min/ 13 stops), exit Gilfaes Turn and then walk about 10 minutes to destination - take care walking along A40 and road to destination.

- Megabus also has a bus that picks up at the University and drops off in Abergavenny, but takes twice as long.

- Estimated travel time: 1 hour 35 minutes

- Bike: NCN Route #8 (5 miles)

Services

- Dogs allowed

- No drones

- Cafe

- Gift Shop

- Toilets

Nearby: Blaenavon Ironworks (25 min/ 13 miles away), The Big Pit (27 min/ 13 miles away) and Llanthony Priory (37 min/ 19 miles away), Brecon Beacons National Park (42 min/ 18 miles away)

Where is this bloody castle?!

Wanting to see every castle in Wales is no small task, especially since not every structure has public access, even though they are listed as they do.

Setting off to the town of Llangibby, a mere 30 minute drive from Cardiff, my guy and I talked about the possible difficulty of reaching our goal,

Tregruk Castle. A few nights prior the castle was featured on the TV show Time Travellers here in the UK. The narrator stated that the majority of the Welsh natives have no idea this castle is even here, since it is hidden within a woodland over-growth.

We found the road without a problem, thanks to GPS technology, yet the farmer does not allow public access up the driveway. This important piece of information was not mentioned on the television program. Seeing a footpath sign we parked and searched for an entry along the fence. After a few minutes we gave up hope - there is not an entry point to the trail. We don't give up easily, so we got back into the car and drove to where we thought there might be a side entrance and found what looked to be an old logging road. We parked and hiked for about a mile and decided it was useless when the road started curving away from where we estimated the castle to be. We turned on the GPS to see attractions near us and Usk Castle was located ten minutes up the main road.

Usk Castle

35-minutes from Cardiff, the town of Usk and its castle make a delightful day trip - especially when nearby sites are included. Nowadays, many castles are located on private property and that includes

Usk, yet the family loves showing off their reno-vated castle - just as long that visitors are respect-ful and close the gates.

Park in the free car park, walk past the private residence and up the driveway to the gate that lets you inside the wall. The Keep, a couple of towers, Chapel of St. George and chamber block are still intact. The Keep dates back to 1170, whereas the chamber block is dated 13. The north tower was constructed in 1280, but renovated in 2000. It's a very enjoyable castle, although it's not large, we spent about forty-minutes wandering the grounds. The family has done a fantastic job keep-ing it up and making it a pleasureable visit.

If you are traveling by car and camping along your route, the property offers glamping next to the castle. You can choose to stay in the Shepard's Hut, Medieval Pavillions (tent) or Glyndowr Fort. Call them for information +440750609924 or email THDHUMPRHREYS@yahoo.com

There are footpaths for hiking the countryside as well - the trailhead is located at the back of the parking lot. The village of Usk can be seen in a blink of an eye, but they do have a few nice res-taurants and if you are lucky, a street market with food and craft vendors will be going on.

The chapter photo for Holiday Itinerary was taken from this site.

- Cost: Free

- Open: 10am to dusk, check website for event closure dates
- Parking: Free
- Address: Castle House, Monmouth Rd, Usk, NP15 1SD
- Website: uskcastle.com

How to get there:

- Car: M4 towards Newport, Junction 24 use left lane to exit onto A449 The Midlands/ Monmouth, keep left and follow signs to A449. Take the A472 exit towards Usk/Brynbuga and continue for one mile, turn right at Twyn Square to destination
- Estimated travel time: 35 minutes

Services

- Dogs allowed
- No drone
- No toilets

Nearby: Drive a tank (see *Something Different section), Caerleon Roman Baths, Amphitheatre and Roman Legion (14 min/ 7.9 miles away)

White Castle

Part of the trio that makes up the Monmouthshire

fortresses, White, Grosmont and Skenfrith. White is not really worth going out of your way to see - just the towers and outer wall remain. If you are castle hopping in the area, you might as well add to your itinerary.

There is a walking trail that weaves through the hillside connecting the trio. If you are in the mood for a day hiking (see *Hikes section), then this would be the best reason to see this castle - unless, that is, you would like to hire for a venue.

- Cost: Free
- Open: Year-round, 10am - 4pm
- Parking: Car park
- Address: Abergavenny, NP7 8UD
- Website: cadw.gov.wales

How to get there:

- Car: M4 to Raglan - A449 to Clytha Rd then take Old Abergavenny Rd to White Castle
- Estimated travel time: 1 hour

Services

- Dogs allowed
- No drones
- No toilets

Nearby: SKenfrith Castle (14 min/ 6.8 miles away), Grosmont Castle (17 min/ 7.3 miles away), Ragland (21 min/ 10 miles away), Tintern Abbey (39 min/ 19 miles away)

Weobley Castle

The ruins will not take you long to get through and I suggest passing Weobley Castle, unless you are content taking a meaningless drive.

Small, not exciting and over-priced, this castle will take no time at all going through - in fact, if you have young children, you will spend more time watching the kids roll down the grassy hillside outside the castle.

The best part is the view that overlooks the bay, which is accessible by walking trails that vein through the countryside down to the coast - the trail entrance is located in the parking lot.

- Cadw: Yes

- Cost: Adults £4.20, Children £2.50

- Parking: Free

- Address: Gower Peninsula, Swansea SA3

- Website: cadw.gov.wales

- How to get there:

- Car: M4 to A483 - on the M4 exit junction 47 and take A483/A48 exit to Swansea at the 2nd roundabout take the 2nd exit onto A484, at the roundabout take the 1st exit onto Victoria Rd turn right onto B4295 and stay on until arriving at destination

- Estimated travel time: 1 hour 17 minutes
- Train and Bus: Cardiff Central to Carmarthen (1h 9 min/ 5 stops), exit Gowerton then walk about 7 minutes to Hill Street take bus 116/ Llanrhidian (31 min/ 31 stops), exit Llanrhidian Turn take 115 Landimore (1 min/ 1 stop), exit Greyhound Inn then walk about 16 minutes to your destination
- Estimated travel time: 2 hours 33 minutes

Services

- Dogs Allowed
- No drones
- Gift shop
- Toilets

Nearby: Oxwich Bay Beach (15 min/ 7.4 miles away), Oystermouth Castle (26 min/ 14 miles away), The Mumbles (26 min/ 14 miles away), Coastal Paths

GARDENS & HERITAGE HOMES

The National Trust has taken over a large amount of properties, keeping up the maintenance for public enjoyment. There is a pass available for their properties - at the steep price of £69 for an individual and £116 for two adults. Unless you are planning on visiting more than six or seven National Trust sights, then it is not in your best interest. The National Trust has 300 properties all over the United Kingdom - if you are in the UK for a few months or you live there, the pass might be worth purchasing.

Aberglasney Gardens

It is said that the fully restored garden is the finest in Wales. We just happened to come upon the tourist sign while driving from Dryslwyn Castle to Dinefwr Castle; I recognized the name from the previous night when I was doing research on where we haven't been yet. Since it was mid-February and Wales had been experiencing extreme wind and rain storms continueously for two weeks - I put the thought of visiting a garden out of mind.

As I mentioned, we saw the road sign so we took the turn off, it is located only about two minutes off the main road. We parked the car and looked at the sky - the weather was holding. At the entrance gate we read the property information and we both agreed it was expensive for the time of year. We saw no reason to pay full price for the majority of the outdoor garden not in bloom. This sight is definetly one to visit during the warmer months.

Aberglasney has been made popular by being the setting for the BBC's "*A Garden Lost In Time*". I imagine this garden is delightful with its Yew Tree Arch and award-winning subtropical garden, not to mention, it's rare plants and woodlands. We do plan on returning when the season is appropriate.

Of course, every magnificent garden must have a mansion attached to it; Aberglasney's ground floor has been restored to its grandeur.

- National Trust: Yes
- Cost: Adult £8.09 (odd amount, but with voluntary donation it is £8.90), Children up to 16 are Free
- Open: April - October 10am - 6pm, November - March 10:30am - 4pm
- Parking: free
- Address: Llangathen, Carmarthenshire, SA32 8QH
- Website: aberglasney.org

How to get there:

- Car: M4 to Pen-y-Bont/Bridgend, take A48 then A476/Llandeilo Rd follow road and you will see the brown tourist sign to destination

- Estimated travel time: 1 hour 18 minutes

Services

- Dogs not allowed, with exception to guide dogs

- No drones

- Cafe

- Gift shop

- Toilets

Nearby: Dryslwyn Castle (5min/ 3 miles away), Paxton's Tower (12 min/ 5.9 miles away) - in the opposite direction, Dinefwr Castle and Newton House (11 min/ 4.6 miles away), Carreg Cennen Castle (17 min/ 8 miles away)

Dewstow Garden and Grotto

The only one known in the world, this artificial grotto was built around 1895 and over time it became buried and forgotten. Rediscovered in 2000, this family run subterranean garden is a fun maze to wander - it has a variety of plants and numerous ponds.

The upper ground landscape offers rock gardens, ponds, ornamental areas, seasonal shrubs and flowers and trees from around the world. I highly recommend springtime to see the tulips.

The chapter photo was captured in this garden.

- Cost: Adults £7.50, Children £4.50 (11 - 18),

Children£2.50(6-10)

Kids under 5 - free

Family(2Adults+3Children)£24
    Season Tickets - Single - £25 & Family Season Tickets £50

- Open: Seasonal - Spring to Autumn, check website for open dates and hours

- Parking: free

- Address: Dewstow House, Caerwent, Caldicot, NP26 5AH

- Website: dewstowgardens.co.uk

How to get there:

- Car: M4 towards Newport, at junction 24, use 2nd from left lane and take A449/A48, exit M50/The Midlands/Newport/Monmouth - use right lane to keep right at the fork, follow signs A48/Langstone, at roundabouts keep towards A48, stay on A48 until roundabout Chepstow Rd exit, continue A48, right turn, right turn, right turn onto Dewstow Rd, then left to gardens

- Estimated travel time: 35 minutes

- Train: Cardiff Central to Plymouth, GWR, (24 min/ 2 stops), Exit Severn Tunnel Junction, walk about 35 minutes to destination (Station Rd, at roundabout go right to 1st exit, follow street to B4245, turn right onto B4245 then at the Y keep left onto Dewstow Rd).

- Estimated travel time: 1 hour

- Uber: From downtown Cardiff, £36 - £47+

Services

- No Dogs Allowed - Guide dogs are exempt
- Cafe
- Gift shop
- Toilets

Nearby: Caerleon Roman Baths - Amphitheatre and National Roman Legion (11 miles), Chepstow Castle (6.5 miles)

I highly recommend the Dewstow Gardens and Grotto

Dyffryn Gardens

Splendid gardens to wander, especially during the spring and summer when flowers are in full bloom. If you happen to visit during winter, the bare grounds are still a pleasure to roam and the cafe's cakes are delicious. Step back in time inside the mansion and brush up on Welsh history and the lives of its former owners - knowledgeable volunteer staff located in each room to answer your questions.

- National Trust: Yes
- Cost: Adults £12.00, Child £6.00, Family (1 adult) £20.00 and Family (2 adults) £33.00
- Open: Garden 10am - 6pm (free); House, shop and tea-room please check website
- Parking: Free
- Address: Dyffryn Cl, St Nicholas, Vale of Glamorgan, CF5 6SU
- Website: nationaltrust.org.uk

How to get there:

- Car: M4 to Junction 33, then onto A4232 towards Barry. Exit A48 to Cowbridge. In St Nicholas village follow signs for Dyffryn
- Estimated travel time: 20 minutes
- Bus: X2 bus to St Nicholas, then walk about 1 mile along the road to destination
- Estimated travel time: 45 minutes

Services

- Dogs not allowed

- Cafe
- Gift shop
- Uber: from Cardiff, 20 min/ £16 - £20

Nearby: Tinkinswood Burial Chambers (2 min /.6 miles away), St. Lytha's Burial Chamber (3 min/ .8 miles away), and Old Beaupre' Castle (15 min/ 7.4 miles away)

Insole Court

Newly refurbished Gothic Victorian mansion in the heart of Cardiff. When you enter take a look at the fireplace mantle, you will see hand drawings on either side. There are enough oddities and pleasant touches to this stately home, along with the lovely garden, to make it worth seeing.

- Cost: Free, takes Donations
- Open: 10am - 4pm
- Parking: Free
- Address: Insole Court Fairwater Road, Llandaff, Cardiff, CF5 2LN

How to get there:

- Car: From Cardiff Castle, head west on Castle St/A4161, turn right onto Cathedral Rd/A4119, after 1 mile, turn right onto Cardiff Rd/A4119, then left onto Fairwater Rd, then left to Insole Court

- Estimated travel time: 9 minutes

-     Bus: Castle Stop KA - bus 21/Rhiwbina (6 min/ 6 stops), exit North Road Clinic, transfer, M1/Llandaff (10 min/ 8 stops), exit Heathcock then walk down The Avenue to Fairwater, turn right onto Heol-y-Pavin to Insole Court - the walk takes about 6 minutes

- Estimated travel time: 30 minutes

- Uber: From Cardiff it will cost between £6 - £7

Services

- Dogs not allowed
- No drones
- Toilets

Nearby: Cardiff Castle and Llandaff Cathedral (.38 mile away - walk back the way you came down Heol-y-Pavin straight to Cathedral), Cardiff Bay

National Botanical Gardens of Wales

568 acres of rolling hillside with modern and historic gardens in Carmarthenshire.

I have not been to this garden, but I imagine it's beautiful.

- Cost: Adults £11.50, Child 5.50 (under 5 are Free), Family (one adult) £22 and Family (two adults) £33 - Plus - British Bird of Prey Centre 3.50

- Open: April 1 - Oct 31, 10am - 6pm; Nov 1 - March 31, 10am - 4pm

- Parking: Car park

- Address: Llanarthne, Carmarthenshire, SA32 8HN

- Website: botanicgardens.wales

How to get there:

- Car: M4 to Pen-y-Bont/Bridgend, take M4 to A48, at roundabouts exit towards A48.Take exit B4310 towards Nantgaregig/Porthyrhyd, then left onto B4310, continue straight on B4310, at the roundabout take 2nd exit to destination on the left

- Estimated travel time: 1 hour 6 minutes

- Train: Cardiff Central/Pembroke Dock (2h 6min/ 16 stops), exit Carmarthen, walk to bus station, take bus 195/Llaneilli, ride 18 min/13 stops, exit School, walk about 1 minute to Bancffosfelin, take bus 166/Carmarthen (31 min/ 26 stops), exit Middle Hall then walk (first exit at roundabout) about straight for about 4 minutes to garden

- Estimated travel time: 3 hour 45 minutes

- Bus: Cardiff to Carmarthen, then take bus 195/Llaneilli, ride 18 min/13 stops, exit School, walk about 1 minute to Bancffosfelin, take bus 166/Carmarthen (31 min/ 26 stops), exit Middle Hall then walk (first exit at round-about) about straight for about 4 minutes to garden. The garden website states limited bus service from Carmarthen - and their direc-tions say to take the 279 bus from Carmara-then bus station, but Google Maps provided above route

- Cycle: The National Cycle Network route 47 - the Carmarthen-Llaneli loop (better known as the Celtic Trail) passes by the gardens en-trance.

Services

- Dogs not allowed

- No drones

- Cafe

- Gift shop

- Toilets

Nearby: Carmarthen Castle (12 min/ 9 miles away), Paxton's Tower (8 min/ 3 miles away), Dryslwyn Castle (10 min/ 4.5 miles away), Aber-glasney Gardens (15 min/ 7.8 miles away), Dinefwr Castle and Newton House (23 min/ 11 miles away)

Newton House

Like most of us, the Rhys family had experienced good times and bad over a 300 year period. In 1990 the National Trust took ownership of Newton House to save it. The estate consist of 800 acres that sheep graze and has it's own castle (Dinefwr).

For those of you who are ghost hunters, apparently, this house is haunted - it has been recorded having the most activity in Wales.

You can visit Dinefwr Castle and Dinefwr Park for free - just park outside the gate (or park where we did inside the gate- explained in Dinefwr Castle information).

I have not been inside this stately home.

- Cost: Adults £8.50, Children £4.50, Family £20
- Open: 10am - 5pm, exception during winter, 11am - 3pm
- Parking: Car park
- Address: Llandeilo, Carmarthenshire, SA19 6RT
- Website: nationaltrust.org.uk

How to get there:

- Car: M4 then continue onto A483
- Estimated travel time: 1 hour 30 minutes

Services

- Dogs not allowed
- Cafe
- Gift shop
- Toilets

Nearby: Dinefwr Castle - on the estate property

Tredegar House

17th-century mansion, occupied by the Morgan family for over 500 years. Knowledgeable volunteer staff available to answer your questions and are happy to tell tales of scandals that happened within the walls.

Beautiful gardens to explore - best viewed during warmer months, yet open year-round. Cafe offers tasty treats plus warm and cold drinks.

- National Trust: Yes
- Cost: Adults £10.10, Children £5.05, Family £25.25
- Open: House and Garden: winter 11am - 4pm - all other seasons 11am - 5pm, The shop and tea-room are open yearly 10am - 4pm - check

website for holiday closures

- Parking: Car park pay and display
- Address: Pencarn Way, Newport, NP10 8YW
- Website: nationaltrust.org.uk

How to get there:

- Car: Follow A4161 to Rover Way, turn right, at roundabout take 1st exit, next round-about take 2nd exit - Lamby Way then next roundabout continue straight onto Wentloog Ave, stay on Wentloog Ave/B4239 - continue B4239, left onto Morgan Way, Left on Duffryn Way then at roundabout take 2nd exit onto Pencarn Way, stay on Pencarn Way, taking a left then a series of right turns to destination

- Estimated travel time: 22 minutes

- Train: Cardiff Central - London Paddington, GWR, (10 min/ 1 stop), exit Newport then you have to take an Uber to destination (Uber cost £12 - £15)

- Estimated travel time: 30 minutes

- Bus: Local bus 30, exit Cleppa Park then walk about 15 minutes to destination

- Estimated travel time: 50 minutes

Services

- Dog not allowed
- No drones

- Cafe
- Gift shop
- Toilets

Nearby: Caerleon - Roman Baths, Amphitheatre and Roman Legion (18 min/ 7.6 miles away), Dewstow Gardens and Grotto (25 min/ 17 miles away), Raglan Castle (28 min/ 22 miles away)

HIKES

Walk Wales! There are 870 miles of coastal paths that allows you to cover the coast on foot. Not only will you bask in the beauty that the land and sea offers, but there are many castles and abbeys not far off the trail. The paths are clearly marked and for the most part hug the coastline. Since the trails run between villages, it is easy to stay a night or two before heading onwards. Once you have reached your final destination, hop on a bus back to your starting point.

The entire Pembrokeshire Coast has it's own bus service for trail walkers. It's a hail and ride program, which means, when you see the bus with the cute name, such as: "Poppit Rocket" or "Puffin Shuttle" - just stick out your hand and the driver will be glad to stop and give you a lift back. They are also happy to have your dog on-board. This service runs seven days a week during the summer (May to September) and then two days a week the rest of the year.

Check out the website: visitPembrokeshire.com/ explore-pembrokeshire/getting-around for more information on these special bus services.

The National Trust website breaks down each coastal trail for you to plan your day: effort level, hours, miles, a map, step-by-step instructions with photographs and location directions. There is little to no chance of getting lost once you are on the route: people gates and trail name signs are easily seen at each junction.

Check out the website: nationaltrust.org.uk/ coastal-walks-wales

Brecon Beacon Waterfall Hikes

Numerous dirt paths weave through the national park leading you to waterfalls; while the majority are not very high, the cascading waters are an enjoyable view. If the weather hasn't been dry for a while then expect extreme mud. Many paths are challenging due to steepness, even the stairs are about triple the height of normal. I am not ashamed to say I had to stop more than once to catch my breath and I think I am in decent shape.

Check out the Brecon Beacon website to find your preferred walk and all information needed: hike distance grade, starting point, grid reference.

- Cost: Free
- Open: year-round, check weather forecast
- Parking - Parking attendant on site - cost unsure
- Address: Libanus, Brecon, LD3 8ER
- Website: breconbeacons.org

How to get there:

- Car: Take the A470 - at each roundabout take 2nd exit, staying on A470/North Rd to Brecon Beacon National Park.
- Estimated travel time: 55 minutes

Services

- Dogs allowed

- Toilets

Nearby: Brecon Mountain Railway (43 min/ 21 miles away), Pen-y-Fan (40 min/ 1.7 miles away)

Cosmeston Lake Country Park and Medieval Village

Located 7 miles from Cardiff, Cosmeston Lake is completely accessible and a pleasant walk around the entire lake. The dirt trails zigzag through woods and are popular with dog walkers and joggers.

The majority of dog owners do take responsiblity in cleaning up after their fur babies, but like in most parts of Wales, trash cans to dispose of the poop bags are not to be found - so expect to find little black plastic bags scattered along the trails or hanging from tree limbs. I guess it's people's way of protesting not having anywhere to dispose of their dog feces.

The website states "there is a medieval village that takes you back to the year 1350"; but I had no idea it was there when I was at the park. Now that I do, I will have to go back and find it. Situations like this is the exact reason why I wrote this book - so that you will not miss out.

The village is open 7 days per week.

- Cost: Free

- Open: park year-round
- Parking: Free
- Address: Lavernock Rd, Penarth, CF64 5UB
- Website: valeofglamorgan.gov.uk

How to get there:

- Car: Drive from Duke Street Arcade - A4161 -to Leckwith Rd/B4267 then at roundabout, take the 3rd exit staying on Leckwith Rd, turn right onto Cardiff Rd/A4055 then left on Redlands Rd/B4267 to destination
- Estimated travel time: 25 minutes
- Bus: from Wood St take bus 94/Barry Dock (33 min/ 26 stops) - runs every 40 minutes, exit Cosmeston Lakes then walk about 4 minutes to destination - walking south on Lavernock Rd/B4267, right, right then left
- Estimated travel time: 40 minutes

Services

- Dogs allowed
- Toilets

Nearby: Barry Island Amusement Park (15 min/ 7 miles away), St Fagans National Museum (19 min/ 10 miles away), Penarth Pier (5 min/ 1.7 miles away)

Fforest Fawr

Near the village of Tongwynlais and Pontypridd. Sadly, due to disease - logging has cleared out a portion of the forest, but don't let that stop you from walking or biking the paths after you visit Castle Coch.

- Cost: Free
- Open: year-round
- Parking: Free at Castle Coch

Address: Castle Coch

How to get there:

- Car: Exit the M4 at Junction 32 onto A470, follow signs for castle

- Estimated travel time: 30 minutes

- Train: Cardiff Central/Aberdare (18 min/5 stops), exit Taffs Well, walk about 30 minutes to destination - walk south-east, right onto Cardiff Rd, stay on Cardiff Rd, turning left, then left on Cemetery Rd, right onto Abbey Cl, right onto Taff Trail then left

- Estimated travel time: 45 minutes

- Bus: 132 Gold/ Maerdy - runs every 30 minutes from Cardiff (Sundays every 60 minutes). Exit Bute Street and walk 24 minutes to Castell Coch, then enter park next to the castle

- Bus information: traveline-cymru.info/
- Estimated travel time: 50 minutes

Services

- Dogs allowed

Nearby: Castell Coch (right there next to forest), Caerphilly Castle (12 min/ 4.2 miles away)

Parc Cefn Onn

This 30 acre park is more popular with the locals than tourist, but if you would like to take a break from the city and get back in nature without going far, Parc Cefn Onn trails will take you past streams and ponds, over hills and through woodlands. If you do not have a car, no problem, it's accessable by train - get off at the Lisvane & Thornhill station.

- Cost: Free
- Open: year-round
- Parking: Free
- Address: Lisvane, Cardiff, CF14 0EP
- Website: cardiffparks.org.uk

How to get there:

- Car: Follow A470/North Rd, slight left onto Caerphilly Rd/A469, then at roundabout take the 2nd exit to Excalibur Dr, staying on Excalibur Drive to destination

- Estimated travel time: 18 minutes

- Train: Cardiff Central/ Bargoed (13 min/ 4 stops), exit Lisvane & Thornhill, then walk north onto Cherry Orchard Rd for about 5 minutes to destination

- Estimated travel time: 18 minutes

Services

- Dogs allowed

- Toilets

Nearby: Cardiff Castle (14 min/ 5.8 miles away), St Fagans National Museum (19 min/ 7.9 miles away), Caerphilly Castle (10 min/ 4 miles away)

Pen-y-Fan

Highest peak in South Wales at 886 meters above sea level and is part of the Brecon Beacons National Park. It's a popular hike with gorgeous views of the surrounding valley on a clear day. In Wales there are not many days the weatherman can say "clear and sunny" for the Brecon Beacons. I had to visit the country three times before I had a nice enough day to hike, which of course, brought out everyone else who loves to hike. Regardless how warm it feels when you are at your car, the wind can be blowing once you reach the top and temperatures will drop - expect really strong and cold wind. In early spring I wore two hoodies and a light weight non-breathable raincoat type jacket and I was still a tad chilled - until we left the peak.

There are numerous ways to the top, my guy and I chose the 3-hour route, starting to the left of Storey Arms, which was steep enough to make me feel more accomplished than if I started on the beginners route, that is located to the right of the building. If you take the beginning route up and back, the time estimate is 2 hours. The two paths link together, making one big loop.

If you prefer not to be around swarms of people, there are plenty of other trails to choose from. Pick a hill and go, literally. The majority of hills are bare, unfortunately past Welshman didn't think of replanting new trees, so you will get a great view from any path you take.

Brecon Beacon is known for a sad story that took place August 4, 1900, when five-year-old Tommy Jones disappeared. On that day, Tommy and his father were on their way to visit Tommy's grandparents and the duo stopped in the town near the farmstead before going onward. While they were in town, the two happened to see Tommy's grandfather and his twelve-year-old cousin Willie who were getting supplies. Tommy's grandfather asked

Willie to run ahead and give word that the two had arrived. Young Tommy wanted to go too, so off he went with his cousin, but then he got scared and wanted to go back to his dad. The boys went their separate ways - that was the last sighting of Tommy alive. The whole community searched for the young lad, by the time Tommy was found it was too late. There is a memorial statue for the boy; follow the path along the ridge line to the left when you reach the junction, from either trail behind Storey Arms.

The chapter photo is this site.

- Cost: Free
- Open: Year-round, check weather forecast
- Parking: Roadside and car park
- Addresse: Pen-y-Fan, Brecon, LD3 8NF

How to get there:

- Car: A470 to Powys - A470/North Rd, use left 3 lanes to slight left onto Merythyr Rd/A470 - at each roundabout, take 2nd exit until you reach your destination located on right side of street. Unless you're the first there, you will see a lot of cars parked along the side of the road and Storey Arms.
- Estimated travel time: 45 minutes

Services

- Dogs allowed

- Food stands
- Toilets

Nearby: Brecon Beacon Waterfalls (40 min/ 1.7 miles away)

Three Castle Walk

The *Three Castle* walk, 18.6 miles, is recommended to start at White Castle. The White - Skenfrith - Grosmont loop will give you fantastic views of The Marches. In terms of coolness, none of these will "wow" you, especially Skenfrith, but they are an added bonus on your walk.

- Cost: Free
- Parking: Street
- Address: see castles: White, Skenfrith, Grosmont - pick your starting point
- Website: Trail information: abergavenny.org.uk

Services

- Dogs allowed

Nearby: Without doing the 18 mile walk, the Three Castles can be added easily to: Chepstow, Tintern Abbey, Ragland and Goodrich Castle - which is located across the English border and is well worth a visit.

Welsh Wildlife Centre

A nice place to enjoy a nature walk and bird-watching in marsh land: Herons, Buzzards, Geese, Kingfisher and a variety of tweety birds. I have not been here, but the reviews say there are water-buffalo and otters to be seen. The centre has four marked walking paths that vary in degree of difficulty for walking and cycling and a few mobility accessible paths.

- Cost: Free
- Open: 10am - 4pm
- Parking: £3
- Address: Cilgerran, SA43 2TB
- Website: welshwildlife.org

How to get there:

- Car: M4 to Pen-y-Bont/Bridgend, at roundabout take 2nd exit onto A48, keep on A48 until you come to roundabout that has exit A40, then at roundabout for B4298 take that exit, continue for about 15 miles, left on B4332, then right on A478 to Cilgerran Rd follow to destination
- Estimated travel time: 2 hours

Services

- Dogs allowed

- Cafe
- Toilets

Nearby: Cilgerran Castle (6 min/ 1.8 miles away), Cardigan Castle (11 min/ 4.2 miles away), Castell Henllys Iron Age Village (19 min/ 8.8 miles away), Fishguard (34 min/ 20 miles away)

MUSEUMS

Wales has many museums that are not only educational, but can be enjoyed by the whole family. In this section I bypass the art museums and shed light on historic Welsh living - you are bound to be amused.

Aberdulais Falls and Tinplate Works

This little known tinplate factory that used the power of the Aberdulais waterfall was a delightful surprise for not just me, but also for my Welsh partner, who was never taught in school that the tinplate industry started in Wales. Apparently, those employed in the industry were considered lucky - even with having to endure 100°f heat during the duration of their 12-hour shift.

- National Trust: Yes
- Cost: Adult £6.85, Child £3.45, Family £17.05
- Open: 10am - 4pm daily; Mid-February - end of October open 7 days a week, except during winter - then they are only open on weekends
- Parking: Paved car park
- Address: Main Rd, Aberdulais, Neath, SA10 8EU
- Website: nationaltrust.org.uk

How to get there:

- Car: from Neath - Castle Street to Prince of Wales Dr/B4434, continue to Main Rd/A4109 in Aberdulais
- Estimated travel time: 7 minutes
- Bus: Neath, TrawsCymru T6/ Brecon (6 minutes/ non-stop), exit Aberdulais Falls

- Estimated travel time: 1 hour

Services

- Dogs allowed
- Cafe
- Gift Shop
- Toilets

Nearby: Neath Abbey (4 min/ 2.9 miles away), Swansea Museum (18 min/ 11 miles away), Margam Country Park & Margam Abbey (19 min/ 13 miles away)

Big Pit National Coal Museum

Visiting The Big Pit is an absolute must-do while you are in Wales - unless you are afraid of the dark or claustrophobic. This underground tour is presented by real miners that spent their work day underground working by lamp excavating coal. Not only do you learn about the history of The Big Pit, but you get to hear real work stories from your guide. A very enlightening experience into the brutal life of a coal miner, which usually started at the tender age of five.

Important Anything with a battery is not allowed during the underground tour - *including your cell phone and your watch* - because they can cause a fire. Ladies your handbags are also not allowed, the guide will pass a sack around for everyone to drop their goods in. After the tour you can reclaim your items.

Dress warm! You will be surprised at the drop in temperature as the elevator decends. The further you walk away from the shaft into the tunnels, it gets colder and colder. You might consider wearing gloves too. Don't bother wearing a hat to keep your head warm, hard hats are provided.

The chapter photo is from this site.

- Cost: Free (but worth money if they charged)

- Parking: £3 - pay and display parking lot or if you follow the GPS that takes you to the backside of the Big Pit, there's free parking.

- Open:9:30am-5pm

Underground tours: 10am - 3:30pm

- Address: Blaenafon, Torfaen, NP4 9XP

- Website: museum.wales

How to get there:

- Car: M4 heading east to Newport, at Junction 26 take exit A4051/Newport/Caerleon then at roundabout take the 1st exit onto Malpas Rd/A4051, next roundabout do the same, then the next roundabout exit 3rd exit onto A4042, keeping on A4042 - exiting each roundabout to stay on A4042, then when you come to roundabout with exit A472 take it (2nd exit), stay on A472 until you come to A4073 - 2nd exit at roundabout, keep going and you will see brown tourist signs, turning right onto Prince St/B4346, left on Estate Rd and up to destinataion

- Estimated travel time: 45 minutes

- Train: Cardiff Cental to London Paddington, GWR (9 min/1 stop), exit Newport, walk about 6 minutes to Market Square (Stand 16) and take the X24 gold/Blaenavon (49 min/41 stops), exit Curwood then walk 25 minutes to Big Pit.

- Estimated travel time: 1 hour 55 min

- Bus: National Express, Sophia Gardens, Cardiff to Newport (£3.60/ 35 min). Once in Newport take the X24 gold/Blaenavon, Market Square (Stand 16) (49 min/ 41 stops), exit Curwood then walk 25 minutes to Big Pit.

- Estimated travel time: 2 hours

This is one of the few attractions I will say is 100% worth the hassle taking the train or bus to visit.

Services

- Dogs not allowed
- No drones
- Cafe
- Gift shop

- Toilets

Nearby: Blaenavon Ironworks (3 min/ .8 miles away), and Brecon Mountain Railway (24 min/ 16 miles away), Raglan Castle (25 min/ 16 miles away), Roman Bath, Amphitheater & Roman Legion (29 min/ 15 miles away)

I highly recommend The Big Pit

Blaenavon Ironworks

Seeing what is left of the ironworks buildings makes for an educational day. On the property are cottages that are furnished in time-period pieces, taking you through each era. It's actually mind-blowing seeing how the workers and their families lived.

To make it worth the drive to Blaenavon, be sure to add The Big Pit to your itinerary.

- Cadw: Yes
- Cost: Adults £5.80, Children £3.50, Family £16.80 Seniors £4.60
- Open: Seasonal 10am - 5pm
- Parking: Free
- Address: North Street, Blaenavon, NP4 9RN
- Website: cadw.gov.wales

How to get there:

- Car: M4 heading east to Newport, at Junction 26 take exit A4051/Newport/Caerleon then at roundabout take the 1st exit onto Malpas Rd/A4051, next roundabout do the same, then the next roundabout exit 3rd exit onto A4042, keeping on A4042 - exiting each roundabout to stay on A4042, then when you come to roundabout with exit A472 take it (2nd exit), stay on A472 until you come to A4073 - 2nd exit at roundabout, keep going and you will see brown tourist signs, turning right onto Prince St/B4346 to destination

Estimated travel time: 45 minutes

Train: Cardiff Cental to London Paddington or Nottingham or Manchester Piccadilly (they all stop in Newport), exit Newport, walk about 6 minutes to Market Square (Stand 16) and take the X24 gold/Blaenavon (49 min/ 41 stops), exit Curwood then walk to desination

Estimated travel time: 1 hour 55 min

Bus: National Express, Sophia Gardens, Cardiff to Newport (£3.60/ 35 min). Once in Newport take the X24 gold/Blaenavon, Market Square (Stand 16) (49 min/ 41 stops), exit Curwood then walk to destination

Estimated travel time: 2 hours

Services

- Dogs allowed
- No drones
- Gift shop
- Toilets

Nearby: Pontypool Blaenavon Heritage Railway (2 minutes/ .5 miles away), The Big Pit (3 min/ .8 miles away), Raglan Castle (23 min/ 16 miles away), Roman Baths - Amphitheater & Roman Legion (26 min/ 15 miles away), Dewstow Gardens and Grotto (38 min/ 26 miles away)

Castell Henllys Iron Age Village

Just like St Fagans National History Museum in Cardiff, this Iron Age village has workers performing task. Watch the woodworkers, hear stories or hike the Pembrokeshire Coast National Parks thirty acres. Unlike St Fagans, where properties were dismantled then reconstructed, this village is set upon the original foundations of the Demetae tribe, who lived 2,000 years ago.

I have not been to this living museum yet, but I have been to St Fagans. Unlike Castell Henllys, St Fagans is free and offers more.

- Cost: Adults £5, Child £3, Family £13

Season ticket: Adult £15, Child £12, Family £40

* Season tickets allow access to Carew Castle (50 min/ 21 miles away)

- Open: Daily 11am - 3am, exception December 21 - January 5

- Parking: Car park

- Address: Meline, Pembrokeshire, SA41 3UR

- Website: castellhenllys.com & Pembrokeshirecoast.wales

How to get there:

- Car: M4 to Pen-y-Bont/Bridgend - stay on M4 for 46 miles, at roundabout take 2nd exit onto A48, next roundabout take 2nd exit, keeping on A48, then take 2nd exit at next roundabout onto A40, at following roundabouts keep exiting onto A40, then turn right onto B4298, keep on B4298 turning left and right many times, then turn left onto A487 to destination

- Estimated travel time: 2 hours

Services

- Dogs allowed

- No drones

- Cafe

- Gift shop
- Toilets

Nearby: Dyfed Shire Horse Farm (4 min/ 1.4 miles away), Welsh Wildlife Centre (20 min/ 8.8 miles away), Cilgerran Castle (17 min/ 8.5 miles away), Carew Castle & Tidal Mill (49 min/ 29 miles away)

Cyfarthfa Castle Museum

This castle home was built in 1824 for an iron tycoon's son, William Crawshay II. It cost £30,000 and when his father found out the price tag, William was almost disinherited.

The main floor of the museum displays artwork and an impressive collection of ancient Egyptian artifacts and the basement is full of cultural tools, time period outfits and an abundance of information about the iron industry. Depending on how much information you read will determine the amount of time you will need to plan; schedule a minimum of one hour.

- Cost: Adults £2
- Open: Week days 10am - 5pm - Weekends 12pm - 5pm
- Parking: Pay and Display
- Address: Brecon Rd, Merthyr Tydfil, CF47 8NN

137

- Website: visitmerthyr.co.uk

How to get there:

- Car: Merthyr Rd/A470 - stay on until you reach roundabout with exit onto Swansea Rd/A4102 and keep on A4102 until you reach Cyfarthfa Rd/A4054 stay on A4054 to destination

- Estimated travel time: 35 minutes

- Train: Cardiff Central to Merthyr Tydfil, Transport for Wales, (1hr/ 13 stops), exit Merthyr Tydfil walk 4 minutes to bus station, take bus 27/Gurnos (3 min/ 3 stops), exit St Mary's Church then walk 15 minutes to destination

- Estimated travel time: 1 hour 47 minutes

- Bus: Philharmonic JP bus stop, take the T4 TrawsCymru/Newtown, exit Bus Station and walk 24 minutes to destination

- Estimated travel time: 1 hour 19 minutes

Services

- Gift shop
- Toilets

Nearby: Brecon Mountain Railway (9 min/ 3.3 miles away), Aberdulais Falls and Tinplate works (26 min/ 21 miles away), Neath Abbey (29 min/ 23 miles away)

Neath Abbey Ironworks

There is not a museum here, nor much to see. If you are interested in learning about ironworks, I recommend Blaenavon Ironworks.

- Cost: Free
- Parking: Free
- Address: Neath, SA10 7DW
- Website: cadw.gov.wales

How to get there:

- Car: Car: M4 to exit 43, A465 and continue to roundabout, take 1st exit, A474, continue on A474 - 1st exit toward Neath, take 2nd exit onto Longford Rd to Neath Abbey Ironworks
- Estimated travel time: 1 hour
- Train: Cardiff Central to Milford Haven (44 min/ 4 stops), exit Neath then walk 25 minutes (left on Windor, left on Croft, over Bridge St, left on Neath Abbey Rd/A4230) to destination
- Estimated travel time: 1 hour 10 minutes
- Bus: National Express, Sophia Gardens, Cardiff (£5.30-£6.90/ 55 min) - then walk about 25 minutes (New St turns into Angel St, Angel street bends, then take a right onto Croft Rd,

right onto Bridge St, left on Neath Abbey Rd at roundabout keep to the right, A4230, then right on Heol Longford to destination

- Estimated travel time: 1 hour 30 minutes

Services

- Dogs allowed

Nearby: Aberdulais Falls & Tinplate Works (4 min/ 2.9 miles away), Swansea Museum (21 min/ 11 miles away), Margam Country Park and Abbey (17 min/ 11 miles away), National Botanic Gardens (27 min/ 26 miles away), Carreg Cennen Castle (43 min/ 29 miles away)

St. Fagans National History Museum

Welsh living museum that gives a glimpse into life throughout the ages - educational and fun for the whole family. This museum brings to life Celtic times to present day. The grounds include reconstructed homes and businesses from historical time periods, plus there's a children's carnival, beautiful gardens, educational center, castle (more like an estate home) and plenty more to explore.

This working museum transports you back in time - when life depended on your neighbors skill to provide needs: blacksmith, tanner, cobbler. It's fascinating to watch the craftsmen hard at work.

Food and beverages are available - either in the main building, the onsite traditional 1930's tea-room and also at the castle; fresh bread is for sale at Popty Derwen Bakehouse.

The gift shop located inside the main building offers a variety of Welsh products.

- Cost: Free
- Open: 10am - 5pm daily (open Bank Holiday Mondays)
- Parking: £5, or park for free on the street and walk in
- Address: Cardiff, CF5 6XB
- Website: museum.wales
- How to get there:
- Car: A4161/Duke Street, head south-west, turn right onto Cathedral Rd/A4119, continue straight, Pencisely Rd/B4488, Continue onto St Fagans Rd onto Cardiff Rd, Cardiff Rd will sightly turn left and becomes Castle Hill, continue to destination
- Estimated travel time: 20 minutes
- Train: Cardiff Central/Radyr (7 min/2 stops), exit Waun-gron Park, walk about a minute east towards Fairwater Rd West, at Waungron

Park Station take bus 32A/St Fagans (9 min/8 stops), exit St Fagans Museum - walk about a minute, heading east, then turn left, right, then left to destination

- Estimated travel time: 25 minutes

- Bus: 32A/St Fagans from Westgate St runs every 30 minutes - exit St Fagans Museum - walk about a minute, heading east, then turn left, right, then left to destination

- Estimated travel time: 32 minutes

Services

- Dogs allowed on grounds, but not in historical properties

- Cafe

- Gift shop

- Toilets

Nearby: Insole Court (9min/ 2.4 miles away), Llandaff Cathedral (13 min/ 2.9 miles away), Cardiff Castle (17 min/ 4.5 miles away)

I recommend St. Fagans National History Museum

Roman Baths, Amphitheatre and National Roman Legion Museum

The Romans left their mark all around Wales, while most are not worthy of a stop, the Roman

Fortress Baths and The National Roman Legion Museum in Caerleon should be on your list. The amphitheatre is a couple minutes walk away, but it's nothing to get all excited about.

The Roman Fortress Baths Museum will only take about half an hour, perhaps longer if you read everything, and has some unusual artifacts such as gladiator shoes, wax writing tablets and bathroom supplies. A large non-water filled pool takes up the center of the museum.

After you leave the Roman Baths, turn right and you will find the National Roman Legion Museum a short stroll away. Walk across the street, and turn left, to see the amphitheatre sunken in the field.

Unlike most of the villages throughout Wales where businesses have closed down, here in Caerleon there are plenty of pubs and shops that have enough customers to remain open.

- Cost: Free for the National Roman Legion Museum and Amphitheatre, but - *Roman Baths* cost - Adult £4.20, Children £2.50, Family £12.20

- Open: Monday - Saturday 10am - 5pm, Sunday 12pm - 3pm

- Parking: Pay and Display

- Address: High Street, Caerleon, Newport NP18 1DY

- Website: museum.wales

How to get there:

- Car: M4, forllow to Malpas Rd/A4051 in Newport - exit 26, continue on Malpas Rd then take A4042 and B4596 to High St in Caerleon

- Estimated travel time: 35 minutes

- Train: Cardiff Central/Portsmouth Harbour (12 min/ non-stop), exit Newport, walk to bus taking care due to inadequate road for walking, about 8 minutes - head south east, left onto Queensway/B4591, cross street and take pedestrian overpass, left onto Bridge St, left onto Skinner St, right onto A4042 - Newport Friars Walk (stand 7) take bus 60/Monmouth (9 min/ 7 stops), exit Caerleon walk north-west on High St to destination

- Estimated travel time: 45 minutes

- Bus: Greyfriars Rd GG, take X30/Newport (40 min/ 9 stops), exit Newport Friars Walk (stand 7), then walk 2 minutes to catch the 60/Monmouth (9 min/ 7 stops), walk northeast on Corn St, left towards Skinner St, right onto Skinner St, then right onto A4042 - taking bus 60 - exit Caerleon PO, walk north-west on High St towards Backhall St/Cross Street, 2 minutes to destination

- Estimated travel time: 1 hour

Services

- Dogs not allowed, except at amphitheatre
- Gift shop
- Toilets

Nearby: Dewstow Gardens and Grotto (21 min/ 11 miles away), Raglan Castle (22 min/ 16 miles away), Chepstow Castle (24 min/ 17 miles away)

I recommend the Roman Baths and Legion Museum

Swansea Museum

Wales oldest museum not only displays ancient Welsh artifacts and has an amazing collection of porcelein dishware, but also houses an Egyptian mummy! Hor's tomb came to Wales in the 18th-century by a Welsh tomb raider and is on permanent display at the Swansea Museum. There is enough oddities that makes this museum worth going to - and it's totally worth stopping to see Hor.

- Cost: Free
- Open: 10am - 4:30pm - closed Mondays
- Parking: Street parking - pay and display
- Address: Victoria Rd, Swansea, SA1 1SN
- Website: swanseamuseum.co.uk

How to get there:

- Car: M4 towards Swansea, Junction 42, take A483, exit Swansea - merge onto A483, keep left to merge onto Fabian Way/A483 to destination

- Estimated travel time: 50 minutes

- Train: Cardiff Central to Milford Haven (1h/5 stops), exit Swansea then walk about 15 minutes, along B4489, to destination

- Estimated travel time: 1 hour 15 minutes

- Bus: Cardiff Coach Station, bus 201/Swansea (1hr 10 min/ 3 stops), exit Swansea then walk 8 minutes to destination

- Estimated travel time: 1 hour 20 minutes

Services

- Dogs not allowed

- Gift Shop

- Toilets

Nearby: Oystermouth Castle (15 min/ 5 miles away), The Mumbles (15 min/ 5 miles away), Carmarthen Castle (37 min/ 31 miles away), Aberglasney Gardens (38 min/ 26 miles away), Cerreg Cennen Castle (46 minutes/ 27 miles away)

I highly recommend Swansea Museum

The Royal Mint

Did you know that Britain produces coins for not only the United Kingdom, but also 60 other countries? The tour begins with an educational video, then a guide takes you through the process of coin production, a look inside the factory, and if you pre-bought a coin at time of tour purchase - you get to stamp your own commemorative coin. Then the guide takes you back to the main visitors building to roam the museum on your own.

Purchase tickets and tour time online (recommended) or show up and wait for your time slot to start. I would imagine the month would determine if you need to purchase online before you arrive. We showed up on a late Saturday morning during the spring and we got in the next tour - there were about ten of us in the tour. Learn what materials are used and steps taken to produce coin currency. Photographs are not permitted inside the factory, but okay in the museum.

The gift shop offfers souvenirs for kids of all ages, plus jewelery and collector coins; when I was there they were selling Star Wars, Paddington and Marvel.

- Cost: Adults £13, Children (5-15) £10.50, Seniors & Students £11.50, Souvenir coin (strike yourself) £2

147

- Open: 7 days a week, 9:30am - 4:30pm - Tours start at 10am

- Parking: Free visitor car park

- Address: Pontyclun, CF72 8YT

- Website: royalmint.com

How to get there:

- Car: M4 at Junction 34, take the A4119, exit Llantrisant/Rhondda, at the roundabout take the 3rd exit onto A4119, at each round-about exit onto A4119 then onto Heol-y-Sarn to destination

- Estimated travel time: 25 minutes

- Train: Cardiff Central to Aberdare (25 min/ 6 stops), exit Treforest then walk to Otley Arms, take bus 100/Pontypridd (27 min/ 36 stops), exit Edwards Business Park then walk about 3 minutes to destination

- Estimated travel time: 1 hour 16 minutes

- Bus: Greyfriars Road GE, bus 122/Tonypandy (56 min/ 54 stops), exit Industrial Estate, then walk down Heol-y-Sarn, about 8 minutes to destination

- Estimated travel time: 1 hour 4 minutes

Services

- Cafe
- Gift shop

- Toilets

Nearby: St. Fagans National Museum (19 min/ 9.1 miles away), Llandaff Cathedral (21 min/ 10 miles away), Castle Coch (19 min/ 11 miles away), Caerphilly Castle (20 min/ 12 miles away), Cyfarthfa Castle Museum (34 min/ 20 miles away), Aberdulais Falls and Tinplate Works (39 min/ 35 miles away), Neath Abbey (39 min/ 34 miles away)

I highly recommend The Royal Mint

PARKS AND PIERS

Discover dinosaurs, roam woodlands or hang-out at the seaside. There is a park or pier that will suit your fancy.

Barry Island Amusement Park

An average carnival with games and rides that will entertain children. I preferred walking the nearby coastal path.

- Cost: Various carnival attractions
- Parking: Free on street
- Address: Barry, CF62 5AJ
- Website: visitthevale.com

How to get there:

- Car: From Cardiff Castle, head west on Castle St/A4161, towards Castle Arcade, slight left onto Leckwith Rd/B4267, at roundabout take the 3rd exit to stay on Leckwith Rd, next roundabout take exit Leckwith Rd/B4267, after a mile, slight right onto Pen-y-Turnpike Rd, then left onto Greenfield Ave, right onto Cardiff Rd/A4055 - continue on Cardiff Rd/A4055 all the way, (road names change but remains A40550 - at roundabout with exit Ffordd Y Mileniwn (1st exit), continue on Ffordd Y Mileniwn then left onto Station Approach/A4055 to destination
- Estimated travel time: 25 minutes
- Train: Cardiff Central to Barry Island (29 min/ 8 stops), exit Ynys y Barri/Barry Island, then walk 4 minutes to destination

- Estimated travel time: 40 minutes
- Bus: Cardiff Bride KR bus stop - take bus 96A/ Barry (39 min/ 45 stops), exit Adar Y Mor then walk about 1 minute to destination
- Estimated travel time: 45 minutes

Nearby: St Lythans Burial Chamber 913 min/ 6 miles away), Dyffryn Gardens (15 min/ 6.6 miles away), Tinkinswood Burial Chamber (15 min/ 6.7 miles away), Penarth Pier (19 min/7.6 miles away), Duneraven Bay (33 min/ 19 miles away)

Bute Park

One of the things I love about Cardiff is all the parks. Bute is the main park and is located behind the Cardiff Castle. This 130 acre park is beautifully landscaped and runs along the River Taff. There are three cafe's located within the park, a decent distance from each other - coffee, tea, cakes and ice cream are offered. If you have bicycle you can ride the trail from Cardiff to Castell Coch (taking a short detour through town). I ride my bike often to both castles and it's a very pleasant ride. I would estimate from castle to castle will take about an hour. It is a very popular path with walkers and cyclist, so pay attention - and keep to the left, cyclist can zoom by at high speeds and may cause a collision if you're not careful.

- Cost: Free

- Parking: Pay and Display, parking garage or if you're lucky on a side street
- Address: North Rd, Cardiff, CF10 3ER
- Website: bute-park.com

Services

- Dogs allowed
- Cafes
- Toilets

Nearby: Cardiff Castle (1 minute outside East and South gates), National Museum (3 min/ .5 miles - exit East gate), Cardiff Bay (11 min/ 3.2 miles away)

Cardiff Bay

A great place to spend time eating, drinking and strolling along the bay. Boat rides or renting your own boat is possible. The kids can take a spin on the merry-go-round located near the Millennium Centre or play at the playground that is on the east side of the bay - around a two mile walk. Hiring bicycles is possible. If you get lucky, you might catch the locks being open and closed, letting vessels in and out of the bay.

The chapter photo for Theatre was taken here.

- Cost: Free to walk around
- Parking: Variety - I recommend finding a side street to park for free and walk in. Plenty of parking garages nearby - prices vary and some are criminal
- Address: Bute Pl, Cardiff Bay, CF10
- Website: cardiffbay.co.uk

Nearby: Cardiff Castle (10 min/ 3.3 miles away), Bute Park (10 min/ 3.3 miles away), Penarth Pier (11 min/ 4.4 miles away), St Fagan's National Museum (16 min/ 9.7 miles away), Llandaff Catherdral (18 min/ 5.5 miles away),

Cosmeston Lake Country Park - see section: Hikes

Craig-y-Nos Country Park

Located in the Brecon Beacons, this 1.37 mile walk will take you through Adelina Patti's gardens. Adelina established these gardens around her mansion in the late 19th century.

I haven't been here yet, but it looks like a nice place to stroll on a sunny day.

- Cost: Free

- Open: always
- Parking: Car park
- Address: Pen-y-Cae, Craig-y-Nos, Swansea SA9 1GL
- Website: breconbeacons.org

How to get there:

- Car: Merthyr Rd/A470, stay on A470 until you get to roundabout that has exit for Heads of the Valley Rd/A465, it's the 1st exit, continue on A465 until you get to exit A4109/ Glyn-nedd, continue on A4109 for 7 miles, turn right onto A4067 to destination
- Estimated travel time: 1 hour

Services

- Dogs allowed

Nearby: National Showcaves and Dinosaur Park (3 min/ .8 miles away), Aberdulais Falls and Tinplate Works (24 min/ 13 miles away), Neath Abbey (27 min/ 21 miles away), Swansea Museum (35 min/ 21 miles away), Brecon Mountain Railway (32 min/ 23 miles away)

Folly Farm Animal Park and Zoo

Rhinos, penguins, lions and giraffes are only a few residents that call Folly Farm home. This 120 acre park and zoo is home to 750 animals and also has a vintage fairground with an antique merry-go-round, a giant ferris wheel and theater that houses a Wurlitzer organ - making it a fun-filled day for everyone in the family.

I haven't been to this attraction yet, but if you have young children it sounds like something they would enjoy doing between visiting castles.

- Cost: Adults £16.95, Child £14.95 (3 - 15), Toddler £10.95, Under 2 are Free, Seniors £14.95

- Open: Yearly except major holidays - 10am - 4pm or 5pm depending on season

- Parking: Car park

- Address: Begelly, Kilgetty, Pembrokeshire, SA68 0XA

- Website: folly-farm.co.uk

- How to get there:

- Car: M4 towards Pen-y-Bont/Bridgend, then take A48 to Carmarthen. You will need to then head towards Tenby - At roundabout take 2nd exit onto A40 after 8 miles at roundabout exit 1st exit onto A477, after 12 miles at roundabout exit onto A478 - follow the brown tourist signs to destination.

- Estimated travel time: 1 hour 40 minutes

Services

- Dogs not allowed
- No drones
- Cafe
- Toilets

Nearby: Tenby (12 min/ 6 miles away), Manorbier Castle (21 min/ 11 miles away), Coastal Paths and Beaches, Laugharne Castle (23 min/ 16 miles away)

Margam Country Park

There's something for everyone in Margam Park: childrens fairytale village, adventure park, Go Ape! zip-line experience, gardens, farm animals, train ride, orangery & gardens, walking and biking trails and a magnificent 19th-century Tudor Gothic Castle and cistercian abbey ruins - dating back to 1147. If you have bikes - pack them, this 1000 acre country estate has paved and unpaved trails.

Without joining a tour, entry into the castle is not permitted past the lobby. The ground floor offers historic information and an impressive staircase.

*If you're into Geocaching the park is full of treasures.

Go Ape! - Do you have what it takes to take the leap? The Tarzan swing drops you six meters -

landing you into a cargo net. If the swing is a little too much for your stomach, the Tree Top Challenge's zip-line might be more your style. Go Ape is for ages 10 and older - Children's Adventure Playground is set up for the younger ones.

Pack a picnic or enjoy a beverage and snack at the cafe.

The Ivy Cottage, located across from Margam Abbey, is available for vacation rental and allows access into the park - even while it is closed.

The chapter photo is located within this site.

- Cost: Free - Except during events/bank holidays: Adults £4 - £14, Child £3-£10

- Cost: Go Ape! £33 (16 and older) and £25 (10-15 years old)

  pre-book online and save 20%

- Open: Spring & Summer: 10am - 6pm, Autumn & Winter: 10am - 4pm

- Parking: Car £6, Motorbike £3 - or save your money and park on street outside of gates for free and walk-in.

- There is also free parking along the backside of the park, near the pond and walking trails - set GPS for Margam Abbey. Instead of turning right to the abbey, keep going straight and you will see a parking area beside the pond. Walk up the street and follow the foot-path, to the right, through the forest into Margam Park or walk back down to the abbey and enter the park through its side door.

- Address: Port Talbot, SA13 2TJ
- Website: margamcountrypark.co.uk & goape.co.uk

How to get there:

- Car: M4, at juction 38 exit A48 to Port Talbot, keep on A48 - follow brown tourist signs to destination
- Estimated travel time: 35 minutes
- Train and Bus: Cardiff Central toward Swansea, get off at Pen-y-Bont/Bridgend. Walk about 4 minutes to Bridgend Bus Station (Bay 1) and take the X1 or X4 Swansea, get off at Margam Park. Walk about 7 minutes to Parc Gwledig Margam Country Park
- Estimated travel time: 2 hours

Services

- Dogs allowed
- Cafe
- Toilets

Nearby: Margam Abbey (at property), Neath Abbey (15 min/ 11 miles away), Aberdulais Falls & Tinplate Works (16 min/ 13 miles away), The Royal Mint (27 min/ 24 miles), Swansea Museum (22 min/ 13 miles), The Mumbles (31 min/ 17 miles), Cyfarthfa Castle Museum (39 min/ 33 miles away)

I highly recommend Margam Country Park

National Showcaves and Dinosaur Park

The National Showcaves and Dinosaur park in Dan-yr-Ogof is a great way to spend a rainy day. This is the worlds largest dinosaur park and great fun for all ages. In 1912, the Morgan brothers discovered three caves - Dan-yr-Ogof, Cathedral and the Bone Cave. Cathedral Cave is the largest of the three and can be rented for weddings.

Life-size mechanical dinosaurs, with information plaques, are placed throughout the park trails as you go from cave to cave.

Standing stones and burial chambers are found on the grounds. The park also has a museum, iron age farm, fossil house, panning for gold and a farm that includes Shetland ponies and Shire horses.

We had a great day exploring the caves and learning about some unusual dinosaurs that we've never heard of before. If you have a child who likes dinosaurs, this is the park to bring them.

- Cost: Adults £15, Child £10
- Open: April 1 - November 1, 10am - 3pm

- Parking: Free onsite car park

- Address: Abercraf, Swansea, SA9 1GJ

- Website: showcaves.co.uk

- How to get there:

- Car: Merthyr Rd/A470 continue on A470, exiting each roundabout to stay on A470, when you reach exit for Heads of the Valleys Rd/A465 exit, keep on A465 about 10 miles then take exit A4109/Glyn-nedd/Glynneath/Onllwyn - continue 7 miles, turn right onto A4067, then left and left to destination

- Estimated travel time: 1 hour

- Train: Cardiff Central to Swansea, GWR, (40 min/ 3 stops), exit Neath, then walk to bus stop and wait for bus T6 TransCymru/Brecon (17 min/ 20 stops), exit National Show Caves for Wales, walk 5 minutes to destination

- Estimated travel time: 1 hour 45 minutes

- Bus: National Express, Sophia Gardens, Cardiff to Neath (£5.30 - £6.90/ 55 min), then you need to take the T6 TransCymru/Brecon (17 min/ 20 stops), exit National Show Caves for Wales, walk 5 minutes to destination

- Estimated travel time: 1 hour 20 minutes

Services

- Cafe

- Gift shop
- Toilets

Nearby: Brecon Beacons/Pen-y-Fan (44 min/ 21 miles), Craig-y-Nos Country Park (2 mins/ .8 miles), Swansea Museum (40 mins/ 22 miles)

I highly recommend The National Showcaves & Dinosaur Park

Penarth Pier

First opened in 1898, this fully-restored Victorian era pier allows a nice stroll back to the past with its restored showcase pavillion. It's easy to get to from Cardiff and offers a variety of outdoor venues throughout the summer season.

- Cost: Free
- Open: Daily
- Parking: Street
- Address: Penarth, CF64 3AU
- Website: piers.org.uk

How to get there:

- Car: Cardiff - A4160 - stay on A4160 towards Penarth. At roundabout take 1st exit, then at the next continue straight onto Terra Nova

Way, then at following roundabout take 2nd exit to Penarth Portway to pier

- Estimated travel time: 20 minutes
- Bus: Millennium Center stop, exit Watkiss Way then walk (17 minutes to pier) - go left on the Cardiff Bay Trail, left towards Terra Nova Way, stay on Terra Nova Way, at roundabout 3rd exit, then left, right, left, right to destination
- Estimated travel time: 30 minutes

Services

- Dogs allowed
- Toilets

Nearby: Cosmeston Lakes Country Park (6 min/ 1.7 milesl away), Cardiff Bay (10 min/ 4.2 miles away), Llandaff Cathedral (16 min/ 5.2 miles away), Barry Island (18 min/ 8 miles away), Porthkerry Country Park (21 min/ 11 miles away), Ogmore Castle (34 min/ 24 miles away), Dunraven at Southerndown (38 min/ 26 miles away)

Porthkerry Country Park

If you are into photography and you want to capture an airplane in flight, Porthkerry is right under Cardiff airports landing path. It's a thrill having them fly overhead so close and you can capture some great shots.

220 acres of nature trails through meadowland, woodlands and along the coast - Cold Knap Beach, which is a pebble beach, a cafe, playground, picnic tables and BBQ sites.

- Cost: Free
- Parking: Car park, pay and display
- Address: Park Road, Barry, CF62 3BY
- Website: valeofglamorgan.gov.uk

How to get there:

- Car: Duke St/A4161, head towards Duke St Arcade then turn left onto Leckwith Rd at 3rd roundabout stay on Leckwith Rd/B4276, right onto Pey-y-Turnpike Rd, continue onto Mill Rd/Station Rd and then at roundabout take 1st exit, Ffordd Mileniwm, stay on Ffordd Mileniwm by taking 2nd exit at next round-about and same at the next, the followiing roundabout you will exit the 1st exit onto Broad St/A4055, then Park Rd to Porthkerry Country Park

- Estimated travel time: 35 minutes

- Train: Cardiff Central to Bridgend (24 min/ 7 stops), exit Barry then walk about 25 minutes. From the station take the stairs, head south-west and turn left onto Broad St/ A4055, keep on Broad St by going right and then take a left onto Canon St, turns into Old Village Rd, keep left onto Park Rd which will turn to the right, stay on Park Rd to destination. I estimate it is a couple mile walk down the driveway to arrive at the sea.

- Estimated travel time: 50 minutes

- Bus: Canal St JF stop - T9 TrawsCymru/ Cardiff Airport (27 min/ 6 stops), get off at Cwm Ciddy then walk 14 minutes to the park - north-east on Port Rd/A4226 towards Cwm Ciddy Lane, right onto Cwm Ciddy Ln - stay on Cwm Ciddy Lane - turn left to stay on the lane and then right and a sharp left to destination. Once you enter the property, I estimate it is a couple mile walk to get to the sea.

- Estimated travel time: 50 minutes

Services

- Dogs allowed
- Cafe
- Toilets

Nearby: Barry Island (11 min/ 4.6 miles away), Penarth Pier (20 min/ 11 miles away), St Fagans National Museum (19 min/ 9.7 miles away), Castell Coch (27 min/ 16 miles away), Caerphilly Castle (31 min/ 20 miles away), Ogmore Castle (30 min/ 18 miles away)

Roath Park Conservatory

In its heyday, back in 1894, Roath Park was where the locals swam and tournaments took place. Time period photos are displayed and the park has kept its Victorian-era atmosphere. Plenty of benches to sit line the pathways, encouraging visitors to relax and enjoy for as long as they desire - perhaps with an ice cream cone purchased from the kiosk. Swimming is no longer permitted, but don't let that keep you from enjoying the water - head over to the boatstage/boathouse to hire a rowing boat or pedalo.

- Conservatory: £2 - Open: 10:30am - 3pm Boat or Pedalo: £6 for half-hour, check website for hours
- Parking: Free on street
- Address: Roath Park Botanic Gardens, 170 Lake Rd, East Cardiff, CF23 5PG
- Website: cardiffparks.org.uk

How to get there:

- Car: A4161/North Rd, continue to Corbett Rd, turn right on Corbett Rd, continue to Cathays Terrace, continue onto Fairoak Rd, at the roundabout take 2nd exit staying on Fairoak Rd, then left on Lake Rd East to destination

- Estimated travel time: 10 minutes

- Train: Cardiff Central/Bargoed (9 min/ 2 stops), exit Heath High Level then walk 17 minutes to the park - walking south from Heath Halt Rd towards Lake Rd North, turn left onto Lake Rd North, then right, left and right to the park

- Estimated travel time: 35 minutes

- Bus: From Hayes Bridge Road, bus 28 - 28A/Thornhill (18 min/ 13 stops) runs every 30 minutes - exit Promenade East then walk about 1 minute to the park

- Estimated travel time: 30 minutes

Services

- Dogs allowed in park
- Cafe
- Toilets

Nearby: Cardiff Castle (7 min/ 2.2 miles away), Cardiff Bay (15 min/ 6.5 miles away), Castell Coch (15 min/ 5.3 miles away), Caerphilly Castle (17 min/ 7 miles away), Cyfarthfa Castle Museum (35 min/ 25 miles away)

RELIGIOUS
SIGHTS

King Henry VIII is responsible for the destruction of the religious buildings. He had them destroyed when he seperated himself from the church. These buildings must have been magnificent - what a shame a kings temper tantrum, from not being given the blessing of a divorce, resulted in their mass destruction.

Ewenny Priory

Founded in the 12th century, during the Benedictine order, this priory is unusual due to it's fortified-style, which was not common for Britians religious buildings for that time period.

Today it can be hired as a unique wedding venue. The grounds are open to the public to wander, but if you want to see inside the priory house an advanced appointment is needed.

I have not been to this site.

- Cost: Free, inquiry to enter priory house
- Open: 10am - 4pm daily, except December 24, 25, 26 and January 1
- Parking: Free
- Address: Abbey Rd, Bridgend, CF35 5BW
- Website: ewennypriory.co.uk
- cadw.gov.wales/visit/places-to-visit/ewenny-priory

How to get there:

- Car: You can take either the M4 or A48

- Estimated Travel Time: 40 - 45 minutes

- Train and Bus: Cardiff Central Bridgend (20 minutes non-stop), exit Pen-y-Bont/Bridgend then walk to Station Hill, take bus line 303 Llantwit Major (8 minutes/4 stops) exit Pottery, walk about 16 minutes to Ewenny Priory

- Estimated Travel Time: between 56 minutes and 1 hour 32 minutes

- Bus: X2 Porthcawl from Millennium Centre (46 minutes/ 28 stops) exit College then walk about 3 minutes to Ewenny Road, take bus line 303 Llantwit Major (6 minutes/ 2 stops), exit Pottery then walk about 16 minutes

- Alternative Route: X2 Porthcawl, exit Wyndham Crescent then walk about 41 minutes to priory.

- Estimated Travel Time: 1 hour 30 minutes

Nearby: Ogmore Castle (6 min/ 2.2 miles away), Dunraven Bay at Southerndown (11 min/ 4 miles away), Castell Coch (27 min/ 19 miles away), Barry Island (29 min/ 17 miles away), Caerphilly Castle (32 min/ 23 miles away), Cyfarthfa Castle (48 min/ 38 miles away)

Lamphey Bishop's Palace

Also known as Lamphey Court, this now ruined luxurious medieval palace was used as a retreat for the bishops of St Davids. The monks grew fruits and vegetables and had livestock, which provided them a very wealthy and abundant lifestyle.

What is left of Lamphey might be worth checking out as a time-killer or if you are already in the Tenby area. But, you do not need to go out of your way if you are restricted on time.

- Cadw: Yes
- Cost: Free
- Open: Year-round, 10am - 4pm
- Parking: Car park
- Address: Bishops Palace, Pembroke, SA71 5NT
- Website: cadw.gov.wales

How to get there:

- Car: M4, then take A48 then at the roundabout take the 2nd exit onto A40, next roundabout take the 1st exit and continue onwards to A477. Stay on A477, turn left onto Stephen's Green Lane, then right onto The Ridge-way, then right to your destination

- Estimated travel time: 2 hours

- Train: Cardiff Central to Milford Haven (2h 37 min/ 13 stops), exit Johnston (Pembs), walk to Railway Hotel, take bus 349/Tenby (48 min/ 26 stops), exit Church, walk north on A4139 towards The Ridgeway, turn right onto The Ridgeway, then left to destination

- Estimated travel time: 4 hours 15 minutes

- Bus: From Tenby, Upper Park Road (stop 1) take bus 349/Withybush (38 min/ 21 stops), exit Church, walk north on A4139 towards The Ridgeway, turn right onto The Ridgeway, then left to destination

- Estimated travel time: 45 minutes from Tenby

- There is a bus stop in Manorbier in route to Lampheys Bishops Palace

Services

- Dogs allowed
- No drones
- No toilets

Nearby: Manorbier Castle (12 min/ 4.3 miles away), coastal walk, Presipe Beach (5.3 miles away) Tenby (17 min/ 8.3 miles away), Folly

Farms Adventure Park (17 min / 11 miles away)

Llandaff Cathedral

Definitely worth visiting during your time in Cardiff! If you are like me and enjoy wandering old cemeteries, you will not be disappointed with the onsite graveyard - be sure to walk through the adjacent one too. The cathedral dates back to 1120 and is still used for services today.

- Cost: Free
- Parking: Free
- Open: 9am - 6:30pm daily, except Sunday 7am - 4:30pm
- Address: Cathedral Cl, Cardiff, CF5 2LA
- Website: llandaffcathedral.org.uk

How to get there:

- Car: Head south-west on Duke St/A4161, turn right onto Cathedral Rd/A4119, turn right onto Cardiff Rd, then turn right onto High Street and then turn right onto Cathedral Close
- Estimated Travel Time: 11 minutes
- Bus: Route from Castle Street Stop KB bus line 122 TonyPandy to Black Lion, walk 4 minutes to Llandaff Catherdral. From Black

Lion, walk south-east on Cardiff Rd towards High St, turn left on High Street, then right onto Cathedral Cl

- Estimated Travel Time: 20 - 35 minutes

Services

- Dogs not allowed
- Toilets

Nearby: Insole Court (3 min/ .5 miles away), Cardiff Castle (8 min/ 2.2 miles away), Bute Park (10 min/ 3.1 miles away), Fagan's National Museum (10 min/ 3 miles away), Castell Coch (15 min/ 4.4 miles away), Caerphilly Castle (19 min/ 8.7 miles away)

I highly recommend Llandaff Cathedral

Llanthony Priory

The 12th-century traveler would have had to go a long way into the remote wilderness to come across the monks that called Llanthony Priory home. Tucked away in the Vale of Ewyas, this priory with its extravagant archways must have been a magnificent sight to see after such an enduring journey.

Today, Llanthony Priory is Llanthony Priory Hotel; it might be worth staying a night. I have not visited the ruins nor stayed at the hotel.

- Cadw: Yes
- Cost: Free
- Open: Year-round 10am - 4pm, except December 24, 25, 26 and January 1
- Parking: Car park
- Website: visitwales.com
- Address: Llanvihangel Crucorney, Abergavenny, NP7 7NN
- GPS 51°56'40.7"N3°02'13.0"W

How to get there:

- Car: M4 to Abergavenny then A465 to Llanvihangel-Crucorney
- Estimated travel time: 1 hour
- Train: Cardiff Central to Abergavenny, then walk about 8 minutes to Raglan Terrace, take X3/Hereford (16 min/11 stops) exit Crossways, walk about 3 minutes to destination
- Estimated travel time: 1 hour
- Bus: Mega Bus, Cardiff to Newport (£7.45 / 30 min), exit Gloucher Railway Station, walk south-west out of station entrance, turn right towards Station Approach, continue onto Bruton Way, turn right onto Station Rd. At Station Road (stop Q), take bus 10 gold/Lower Tuffley (8 min/ 5 stops), exit Kwik Fit, then walk north-west on Stroud Rd/

B4072 towards Bristol Rd, then continue on Bristol Road, left on to St Ann Way/A430 then right to destination *use caution - walking route may be not exactly correct

- Estimated travel time: about an hour

Services

- No drones
- Toilets

Nearby: Raglan (32 min/ 21 miles away), Blaenavon Ironworks (34 min/ 19 miles away), Big Pit National Coal Museum (36 min/ 19 miles away)

Margam Abbey

The cisterian ruins are absolutely fantastic and since they are located within the grounds of Margam Country Park, visiting makes an enjoyable outing for the whole family.

* See "Parks" - Margam Country Park

- Cost: Free
- Open: Daily 10am - 4:30pm, November to Mid-January, Monday and Tuesdays open 1pm - 4:30pm
- Parking: Free (if space is not available, drive further up the lane to find free parking near the trail head and pond area). Go through

the Abbey's side door to enter Margam Country Park.

- Address: Neath Port Talbot, SA13 2TA
- Website: margamabbey.co.uk

How to get there:

- Car: M4 from Cardiff
- Estimated Travel Time: 40 minutes
- Train and Bus: Cardiff Central Train Station - toward Swansea - get off at Pen-y-Bont/ Bridgend. Then walk 4 minutes to Bus Station, Bay 2, take X1 or X4 Neath, platform 2. Ride bus for 23 minutes (19 stops). Exit bus at Crematorium stop, walk 8 minutes to Abbey.
- Estimated Travel Time: 1 hour
- Bus: From Cardiff Sophia Gardens bus station, #201 Swansea (every 55 minutes/ 2 stops) exit at Swansea Bus Station (stand 8), walk about 4 minutes to Bus Station (Stand 6), take X1 or X4 Bridgend (ride about 16 - 20 minutes), exit at Crematorium stop
- Estimated Time Travel: 1 hour 20 minutes

Services

- Dogs not allowed
- Toilets

Nearby: Margam Country Park (at property), Neath Abbey (15 min/ 11 miles away), Aberdulais

Falls & Tinplate Works (16 min/ 13 miles away), The Royal Mint (27 min/ 24 miles), Swansea Museum (22 min/ 13 miles), The Mumbles (31 min/ 17 miles), Cyfarthfa Castle Museum (39 min/ 33 miles away)

Neath Abbey

Neath Abbey was once the largest abbey in Wales, that is until Henry VIII had all abbeys destroyed. This ruin does not have the 'wow' factor that Tintern Abbey has, yet the 1129 cistercian monastery is worthy of a stop if for nothing else to see what remains of the once impressive building.

- Cadw: Yes

- Cost: Free

- Open: 10am - 4pm - closed December 24,25,26 and January 1

- Parking: Free on grave road

- Address: Monastery Rd, Neath, SA10 7DW

- Website: cadw.gov.wales

How to get there:

- Car: M4 to exit 42 - the Abbey exit is sign posted. If you miss the exit, continue to exit 43, A465 and continue to roundabout, take

1st exit, A474, continue on A474 - at roundabout take 1st exit, New Rd/A4230 then at next roundabout, take 1st exit onto Monastery Rd, turn left for the Abbey.

- Estimated travel time: 1 hour

- Train: Cardiff Central, the train leaves every 30 minutes (37 min/ 3 stops), exit Castell-Nedd/Neath. Walk about 25 minutes to Abbey

- Estimated travel time: 43 minutes

- Bus: National Express, Sophia Gardens, Cardiff to Neath, it is direct (£6.90). Walk about 25 minutes to Abbey

- Estimated travel time: 55 minutes

Services

- Dogs allowed

- No drones

- No toilets

Nearby: Aberdulais Falls and Tinworks (5 min/ 3 miles away), Swansea Museum (17 min/ 7.7 miles away), Margam Country Park (17 min/ 11 miles away), Cyfarthfa Castle Museum (28 min/ 23 miles away), Paxton's Tower (30 min/ 26 miles away), Dryslwyn Castle (32 min/ 26 miles away), Aberglasney Gardens 34 min/ 27 miles away),

St Davids Bishop Palace

The cathedral of this magnificent medieval palace is one of the highlights of Wales. It is a treasure trove of delightful snapshots for the photographer in all of us. The ceilings throughout the building are phenomenal and each room deserves careful study. I was inside the cathedral for two hours and I could have happily stayed another, if time was on my side.

The chapter photo is from this site.

- Cadw: Yes
- Cost: Cathedral is free - but the remains of the palace has an entrance fee, which I didn't find worth the price. You can see the best parts when you stand at its entrance - the building mimicks the likeness of the majority of castle ruins.
- Cost: Adults: £4.20, Juniors £2.50 (aged 5 - 17), Family £12.20 (admits 2 adults & 3 kids), Seniors £3.50
- Opening Times: July & August: 9:30am - 6pm, September & October: 9:30am - 5pm, November through February: 10am - 4pm
- Address: St Davids, Haverfordwest, SA62 6PE

- Website: cadw.gov.wales

How to get there:

- Car: A487 to St Davids
- Estimated travel time: 2 hours 18 minutes
- Train and Bus: Cardiff Central - Milford Haven (2 h 29 mins/ 12 stops). Get off at Haverfordwest and walk 1 minute to Railway Station - take bus T11 TrawsCymru Connect Fishguard (50 minutes/28 stops), getting off at Nun Street and walk about 8 minutes to destination
- Estimated travel time: 3 hours 54 minutes
- Bus: Haverfordwest - St Davids/Fishguard - Route 413 Fishguard - St Davids
- Estimated travel time: 5 hours 30 minutes

Services

- Dogs allowed
- No Drone
- Gift shop
- Toilets

Nearby: St Non's Chapel & Well (.69 miles - not worth seeing, but coastal walk near it is beautiful), Fishguard (25 min/ 16 miles away)

I highly recommend - the Cathedral is not to be missed

St Dogmael's Abbey and Coach House

What is left standing of the St Dogmael's Abbey is nothing too exciting if you have been to Tintern Abbey - and perhaps even Neath Abbey is more impressive. If you live in South Wales and you are looking for something to do within a couple hours drive or you're a visitor on vacation - the town of Cardigan is delightful and visiting this abbey will be a nice addition to the day. The Coach House is now a museum and visitor center.

- Cost: Free
- Open: Year-round, 10am - 4pm, closed December 24, 25 & 26 and January 1
- Parking: Free
- Address: St Dogmaels, Cardigan, SA43 3DX
- Website: stdogmaelsabbey.org.uk

How to get there:

- Car: Cardigan to St Dogmaels - M4 to B4298 in Carmarthenshire, then take B4299 andn A478 to High Street in St Dogmaels
- Estimated travel time: 2 hours 5 minutes
- Train and Bus: Cardiff Central to Carmarthen (1h 46 min/ 10 stops) in Carmarthen walk to bus stop, about 6 minutes, then take 460 TrawsCymru Connect/Cardigan (1h 34 min/

47 stops) exit Finch Square A, walk 1 minute to Finch Square C - take bus line 408 St Dogmaels (15 min/ 2 stops) to destination

- Estimated travel time: 3 hours 55 minutes

- Bus: National Express - Cardiff Coach Station, Sophia Gardens to St Clears/Carmarthen (£11.20 - £12.90) then walk 1 minute to Rock Cottage and take bus line 322 Haverfordwest (43 minutes/ 13 stops), exit Hospital and walk 2 minutes to Fishguard Road, take T5 TrawsCymru/Aberystwyth (1 h 24 mins/ 27 stops), exit Finch Square C then take bus line 408 St Dogmaels (15 min/ 2 stops) - exit St Dogmaels. *This route stops in Fishguard if you want to plan a stop there to visit this picturesque coastal village

- Estimated travel time: 2 hours 56 minutes

Services

- Dogs allowed

- No drones

Nearby: Cardigan Castle (5 min/ 1.2 miles away), Pentre Ifan Burial Chamber (20 min/ 11 miles away), Cerrag Coetan Arthur Burial Chamber (19 min/ 11 miles away), Fishguard (30 min/ 19 miles away)

Tintern Abbey

Tintern Abbey is well preserved and it is spectacular. The Gothic building dates between the periods of 1131-1536 and offers enough grandeur to make the entrance fee worth paying.

Plan to spend an hour or longer at this site as you discover and learn about its structures and life as a monk. Tours are offered, ask at the desk for next time slot - there are also information plaques provided.

- Cadw: Yes
- Cost: Adults £7.70, Children under 5 Free, Juniors £4.60, Family Ticket £21.60
- Open: 9:30am - 5pm
- Parking: Car park - pay and display
- Address: Tintern, NP16 6SE
- Website: cadw.gov.wales

How to get there:

- Car: M4 and M48 to A466, Cardiff to Wye Valley - Monmouthshire. Take exit 2 from M48 and stay on A466 to Tintern
- Estimated Travel Time: 50 minutes (36.4 miles)
- Train and Bus: Take the train from Cardiff Central to Newport, then take the Severn Express or bus line 16/18/73 - walk to Chepstow

Central Bus Station - take bus line 69 Monmouth, from Chepstow bus station, platform 1, to Tintern Abbey.

- Estimated Travel Time: 1 hour 30 minutes

- Bus: Cardiff Sofia Gardens Bus Station - purchase ticket to Chepstow (£6.60) direct bus and the ride takes 50 minutes. Walk 1 minute from stand 2 to Chepstow Bus Station - stand 1, take bus 69/Monmouth and ride the bus for 15 minutes (13 stops) to Tintern Abbey.

- Estimated Travel Time: 1 hour 20 minutes

- National Express runs the bus line, check their website for schedule to Chepstow

Services

- Dogs allowed
- No drone
- Cafe
- Gift shop
- Toilets

Nearby: Chepstow (14 min/ 5.7 miles away), Dewstow Gardens and Grotto (20 min/ 11 miles away), Raglan Castle (26 min/ 12 miles away) and Goodrich Castle (England - 28 min/ 17 miles away),

I highly recommend Tintern Abbey

SOMETHING
DIFFERENT

E nhance your Welsh experience doing something that you have always wanted to do, but haven't had the opportunity - or see that sight that has a story of it's own.

Dolaucothi Goldmines

Left by the Romans, guided tours take you underground to experience goldmining during the Roman and Victorian era.

I have not been here, but I will as soon as possible.

- National Trust: Yes
- Cost: Adult £10, Child £5.50, Family £25.00
- Open: Check website - the mines open in April and are closed during winter; estate and hiking trails are open year-round, dawn to dusk
- Parking: Free
- Address: Pumsaint, Llanwrda, Carmarthenshire, SA19 8US
- Website: nationaltrust.org.uk

How to get there:

- Car: A470 to A4215 then turn right onto A4067
- Estimated travel time: 1 hour 40 minutes
- Train: Cardiff Central to Milford Haven (2h 7min/19 stops), exit Carmarthen, at Railway Station bus stop take T1 TranwsCymru/ Aberystwyth (1h/40 stops), exit Pioneer, walk 100ft to bus stop Pioneer, take bus 689/

Crug-y-bar (18 min/8 stops), exit Gold Mine and walk a minute to destination

- Estimated travel time: 4 hours 26 minutes

- Bus: National Express to Carmarthen (£7.20/ 2h 10 min) direct, then in Carmarthen, Railway Station bus stop take T1 TranwsCymru/ Aberystwyth (1h/ 40 stops), exit Pioneer, walk 100 feet to bus stop Pioneer, take bus 689/Crug-y-bar (18 min/ 8 stops), exit Gold Mine and walk a minute to destination

- Estimated travel time: 4 hours

Services

- Dogs not allowed
- Cafe
- Gift shop
- Toilets

Nearby: Aberglasney Gardens (27 min/ 17 miles away), Carreg Cennen (33 min/ 18 miles away), Dinefwr Castle (29 min/ 15 miles away), Dryslwyn Castle (30 min/ 19 miles away)

Dyfed Shire Horse Farm

Any horse lover or child will enjoy a day at this farm. Shire horses are "gentle giants" and resemble Clydesdales, if you haven't heard of the breed. The farm gives demonstrations and rides, plus they also have a variety of other kinds of animals on the property. Campsites and cottages are for rent for those who wish to stay overnight or longer.

I have not been to this farm, but it sounds like fun.

- Cost: Adults £7.95, Child £7.45 (under 2 are free), Family £27
- Open: check website
- Parking: Free
- Address: Trelew, Eglwyswrw, Crymych, SA41 3SY
- Website:dyfed-shires.co.uk

How to get there:

- Car: M4 towards Bridgend, then take A48, to A40, right onto B4298, then right onto B4299, continue until you come to A4332, turn left then right onto A478 then left onto B4332, drive 3.4 miles, take a left onto A487 for half a mile then left up the driveway to destination
- Estimated travel time: 2 hours 10 minutes

Nearby: Castell Henllys Iron Age Village (4 min/ 1.4 miles away), Cilgerran Castle (13 min/ 7.1 miles away), Welsh Wildlife Centre (16 min/ 7.4 miles away)

Ianto's Shrine - Torchwood

I have watched a few episodes of Torchwood, but not enough to tell you what's what. Personally, I think a memorial site to a fictional character is odd, but, if you are a Torchwood fan - I imagine you might want to check out Ianto's Shrine wall - just because it's there. Show fans have been leaving notes, pictures and memorabilia on location since the fictional character met his demise.

You can find the shrine down the stairs near Cadwaladers Ice Cream, which by the way is a great place to stop and enjoy a cuppa - tea or coffee, bakery goodies or a scoop.

Cost: Free

Address: Mermaid Quay, Cardiff, CF10 5BZ

Paxton's Tower

This tower overlooks the Towy Valley and River Tywi. Construction started in the early 1800's and finished within a few years. There are two stories told about the tower. The first indicates it was to commemorate Lord Nelson's victories, while the other suggest that Paxton lost an election and to rub the town folks noses in what they could of had - a stone bridge, he built the tower instead. Of course, I am unsure which tale is true.

My beau and I could see the tower looming high

upon a nearby hilltop while we were visiting Dryslwyth Castle, but due to our itinerary being filled, we decided to save it for another day.

That day came during the pandemic when we were given the green light to travel outside our residential area. While it takes only a few minutes to marvel at this lone structure, I recommend visiting for the view. On our visit, fog submerged the valley and it created a breathtaking sight. Off in the distance, Dryslwyth Castle played peek-a-boo through the low hanging clouds.

The photo for Websites Recommended is this site.

- Cost: Free
- Parking: Free - there is a car park near the entrance
- Address: Llanarthney, SA32 8HX
- Website: Nationaltrust.org.uk

How to get there:

- Car: M4 towards Cardiff Airport - take A48 to B4310/Nantgaredig/Porthyrhyd follow to destination
- Estimated travel time: 1 hour 10 minutes

Services

- Dogs allowed
- No drones
- No toilets

Nearby: Dryslwyn Castle (8 min/ 3.5 miles away), Aberglasney Gardens (13 min/ 5.9 miles away), Dinefwr Castle (21 min/ 8.6 miles away), Carreg Cennen Castle (23 min/ 11 miles away), Neath Abbey (31 min/ 25 miles away), Aberdulais Falls (32 min/ 28 miles away), Swansea Museum (35 min/ 26 mile away)

Skomer Island

Puffins! Who can resist hanging out with these adorable birds? Skomer Island is less than a mile off the Pembrokeshire coast and the only way to spend the day, or overnight, on the island is by having a landing ticket - only 250 maximum tickets are sold per day. Pre-booking is not permitted, so you need to be at the Lockley Lodge office way before opening; Peak season is May to Mid-July and can sell out within hours. You might want a back-up plan; island cruises operate allowing you to view the wildlife from the boat - it's only an hour voyage.

Cruises take you around *Skokholm Island* too where thousands of birds colonize: Puffins, Razorbills, Guillemots, Manx Shearwaters and Storm Petrels. No day visitors allowed on Skokholm Island, but you can stay overnight (3, 4 or 7 nights) in an off-the-grid, self-catering 18th-century farmhouse or renovated cowshed. Check website for details.

Boats depart Tuesday to Sunday (closed Monday), times are subject to change. No advanced bookings - Buy your tickets from Lockley Lodge then go down to the boat. Tickets can only be bought on the day and first come, first-served basis.

In December, I checked the upcoming summer season vacancy for an overnight island stay - May, June and July were already fully booked! If you are wanting to stay the night on the island at the hostel accomodations, inquire at least a year in advance.

I haven't done this excursion yet, but it's at the top of my list for when I visit Wales during the appropriate months - when it is up and running.

Important Information

- Lockley Lodge opens at 8am every morning
- **Only cash is accepted to purchase tickets**
- Island is open to visit between either April 1st or Good Friday, whichever comes first, to Mid-September
- Day trip and overnight stays available - limited basis
- The average day trip last only 4 hours
- Boat travel time from shore to island takes about 10 minutes

- Puffins can be seen on the island from April to Aug. In Mid-April you'll have better luck seeing them than at the beginning of the month, where it is a hit or miss. June and July have the biggest numbers and the adults can be seen feeding their single chick.

Lockley Lodge also allocates daily cruise tickets

- No food is available on the island - Lockley Lodge is the last point to purchase snack type foods - bring your own food. Bottled water is available to buy on the island

- Weather determines if the boats are running for the day - check twitter feed for daily updates to make sure boats are going to the island

- Cruise Information: Daily updates on Twitter: @skomer_boatinfo

- Cost: Adult £12, Child £8 - **CASH ONLY** - 1 hour cruise

- Open: Tuesday - Sunday, Closed Mondays - check website for open hours

- Address: Departure, Point Martins Haven, SA62 3BJ

- Website: welshwildlife.org and pembrokeshire-islands.co.uk

How to get there:

Lockley Lodge is located at Martin's Haven, near

Marloes, Pembrokeshire. Haverfordwest/B4327, signposted Dale - follow until you see the Marloes sign. Drive through Marloes village for about 2 miles - park in car park, then from the car park head to lodge which is on the route to boat embarkment for Skomer Island.

Tank School

I haven't done this - yet. But, wouldn't it be amazing!If you would like to drive a tank then sign up for tank school in Usk and have that dream come true. Check out - tankschool.co.uk for more details

Wales Trekking and Riding Association

Horsebacking riding in Wales. I would love to ride along the beach someday - how about you? They have many facilities around the country. Check website for details.

- Website: ridingwales.com

STEAM TRAINS

Seeing the Welsh countryside out the window of a steam train sounds like the beginning of a beautiful day and perhaps it could be - if your expectation is set upon the scenery and not comfort or the length of the trip.

Beacon Mountain Steam Train

I found this train very disappointing and a waste of money. During off-season expect a short forty-five minute round-trip ride, with a half-hour break at the end of the line, so the engine can change direction. A snack shack, picnic tables and restroom facilities are offered at this stop. On the ride back the pace is picked up, so I would say it takes half the time to return.

During the summer another 2-miles is added, but it does not justify the higher price tag, being only a 90-minute round-trip ride. Overall, the ride is boring, seating is extremely uncomfortable and when the train is full you will be sitting knee to knee, touching the person sitting across from you.

Bikes are allowed on the train for a fee, yet with a full car, I cannot see how there could be enough room to accomodate them.

The countryside is beautiful and is loaded with hiking trails, so I recommend instead of taking the train - park your car and hike or cycle the route.

- Cost: General: Adults £15.75, Children £6.50, Seniors £14.25, Dog £3, Bike £3

- High Season & Events: Adults £23.75, Child £14.50, Dog £3, Bike £3

- Open: Weekdays 9am - 2:30pm - Mondays closed - Weekends 9am - 3:45pm

- Parking: Free

- Address: Pontsticill Rd, Pant, CF48 2DD
- Website: bmr.wales

How to get there:

- Car: A470 to Merthyr Tydil, exit towards Pant Estate/Prince Charles Hospital from Heads of the Valleys Rd/A465, then take Bryniau Rd to Pontsticill Rd. The station is 3 miles north of Merthyr Tydfil

- Estimated travel time: 40 minutes

- Train: Cardiff Central to Merthr Tydfil (1h 5 min/ 14 stops), exit Merthyr Tydfil and walk about 5 minutes to Bus Station (Stand 8) and take bus 35/Pant, exit Cemetery Main Gates, walk 7 minutes to destination

- Estimated travel time: 1 hour 45 minutes

- Bus: Castle Stop KA - T4 TrawsCymru/ Merthyr Tydfil (52 min/ 17 stops), exit Bus Station (Stand 16), then walk to Stand 8, take bus 35/Pant (18min/ 23 stops), exit Cemetery Main Gates, walk about 7 minutes to railway station

- Estimated travel time: 1 hour 30 minutes

Services

- Dogs allowed
- Cafe
- Gift shop

- Toilets

Nearby: Cyfarthfa Castle Museum (7 min/ 2.9 miles away), Big Pit National Coal Museum (23 min/ 16 miles away), National Showcaves and Dinosaur Park (35 min/ 24 miles away), Craig-y-nos (32 min/ 23 miles away)

Gwili Steam Railway

Standard Steam railway that runs 4 miles through woodlands. As with the other steam trains in Wales, I wouldn't expect much, but it might be a nice way to spend a couple hours of your day.

I have not taken a ride upon this train.

- Cost: Standard Adult £12 - Steam Sunday Lunch £35 - Santa's Magic Train £12.95, Children Standard £6 - Steam Sunday Lunch £20 - Santa's Magic Train £9.50, Family £31.50 (2 adults + 2 children), Dog £2
- Parking: Car park
- Open: 10am - 5pm, Seasonal, check website
- Address: Bonwydd Arms Railway Station,

Bronwydd Arms

Carmarthen, SA33 6HT

- Website: gwili-railway.co.uk

How to get there:

- Car: M4, continue onto A48. Drive to B4301 in Bronwydd Arms. At roundabout take the 2nd exit onto A48 - stay on A48, taking 3rd exit at next roundabout. After 11 miles you will come to another roundabout, take 3rd exit onto A40, next roundabout take 3rd exit keeping on A40. The next roundabout take 1st exit and again the 1st exit at next roundabout - Dolgwili Rd/A4243 and then the 2nd exit at the following roundabout onto Bronwydd Rd/A484. Turn right onto B4301 to destination

- Estimated travel time: 1 hour 25 minutes

- Train: Cardiff Central/Milford Haven (1h 43 min/ 8 stops) exit Carmarthen, then walk a minute to bus - Railway Station - take bus 460 TrawsCymru Connect/Cardigan (25 min/ 15 stops), exit Bronwydd Arms then walk a few minutes to destination

- Estimated travel time: 2 hour 20minutes

- Bus: National Express, Sophia Gardens, Cardiff to Carmarthen (£13.20 2h 55 min), then - Bus Station (Bay 9) take bus 460 TrawsCymru Connect/Cardigan (12 min/ 4 stops), exit Bronwydd Arms, walk to destination

- Estimated travel time: 3 hours 15 minutes

Services
- Cafe

- Gift shop
- Toilets

Nearby: Camarthen Castle (8 min/ 3.3 miles away), National Botanic Gardens (17 min/ 13 miles away), Dryslwyn Castle (18 min/ 12 miles away), Aberglasney Gardens (19 min/ 13 miles away), Dinefwr Castle (27 min/ 17 miles away), Carreg Cennen Castle (35 min/ 21 miles away)

The Pontypool and Blaenavon Heritage Railway

Steam and diesel locomotives pass through the Brecon Beacons, along side rolling hills and the Garn Lakes. Like most preserved railways, events are hosted throughout the year, such as a 40's weekend and Santa's Grotto during the holiday season.

- Cost: Vary per train: Adult £9 - £10, Children £5- £6 (3 - 15), Family £23 - £25
- Fares allow all day rides, feel free to wander at the drop off areas and then when you are done, get back onboard
- Open: check website for details

    Weekends between Easter and September, Selected Wednesdays during July and August and certain days in October and December
- Parking: Car park, pay and display across the

street from Ironworks

- Address: Blaenavon, Pontypool, NP4 9BE
- Website: pbrly.co.uk

How to get there:

- Car: M4 to exit 26, continue on A4051 to A472 then take A4043 to Blaenavon - located on main road
- Estimated travel time: 50 minutes
- Train: Cardiff Central/Abergavenny (28 min/ 2 stops), exit Cwmbran and walk about 5 minutes to Llantarnam Grange, take bus X24 Gold/Blaenavon (38 min/ 34 stops), exit at Cemetery then walk about 18 minutes to destination
- Estimated travel time: 1 hour 40 minutes
- Bus: National Express, Sophia Gardens, Cardiff to Newport (£3.60/ 30 min), then in Newport, Market Square (stand 16) take the X24 gold/Blaenavon (59 min/ 40 stops), exit at Cemetery, then walk about 18 minutes to destination
- Estimated travel time: 1 hour 45 minutes

Services

- Cafe
- Gift shop
- Toilets

Nearby: World Heritage Center (2 min/ .2 miles away), Blaenavon Ironworks (3 min/ .6 miles away), Big Pit National Coal Musuem (5 min/ 1.2 miles away), Cyfarthfa Castle Museum (25 min/ 17 miles away), Grosmont Castle (34 min/ 19 miles away), Brecon Beacons National Park (38 min/ 27 miles away)

THEATRE

Q uality productions come to Cardiff and if plan ahead, you might catch that show that you have been dying to see.

New Theater

Built in 1906, this theatre presents plays, musicals, dance and children's shows. Check out their website to see what's playing during your visit.

I have not been to this facility yet, unfortunately, every production I've wanted to see has been put on while I was out of the country.

- Cost: Depending on production
- Parking: Parking Garage
- Address: Park Pl, Cardiff, CF10 3LN
- Website: newtheatercardiff.co.uk

Wales Millennium Centre

Not only can you see productions here, the Millennium Centre is also an art center. Often you can listen to a free concert given in the lobby during weekends.

If you have time to take in a musical or concert the Millennium Centre has the perfect seat. Even if you purchase in the "nose-bleed" section, you will have an unobstructed view, regardless of it's price. My guy and I saw Motown here and booked front row in the cheap seats - upper deck, middle of the aisle; our opinion - it was a great location to sit. We were high enough to see all sections of the stage and we could still see the actors faces just fine.

- Cost: Depending on production

- Parking: Many parking garages nearby, but watch out, some do not display price until you are at toll gate and they can run up to £5 per hour - ouch! You might want to park for free on a side street and walk in - just check signs for resident parking only.

- Address: Bute Pl, Cardiff Bay, CF10 5AL

- Website: wmc.org.uk

Services

- Cafe

- Gift shop

- Toilets

- Free concerts in lobby

HOLIDAY
ITINERARY

Once you leave Cardiff your overnight stay options become limited, especially during the high season - plan and book your accomodations early. The majority of "sights of interest" can be made on a day trip from the capital city, yet - driving back and forth to spend the night is not the most effective way to use your time. The list below are towns that are worth staying a night or two; they are also the top holiday spots for the British during the summer, so expect it to be overly populated.

Cardiff to The Mumbles

How to get there:

Car: Take the A470 to the M4 and stay on until junction 42, exit onto A483, keeping left. Follow Fabian Way/A483 and A4067 to The Mumbles

Estimated travel time: 1 hour 8 minutes

Train: Cardiff Central to Swansea (52 min/ 4 stops) then walk to High Street Station take the #4 Metro/Singleton (18 min/ 7 stops), exit Cricket Ground then take bus 2/Newton (13 min/ 10 stops), exit at Oystermouth Square.

Estimated travel time: 1 hour 40 minutes

Bus: National Express, Sophia Gardens, Cardiff to Swansea (£5.30 about 1h 15min), exit Port Talbot Parkway, walk about 2 minutes to Port Talbot Parkway (Stand 6), take bus X3 Cymru Clipper (33 min/ 21 stops), exit Bus Station (Stand G) walk to Stand W, bus 2C/Caswell Bay (21 min/ 14 stops) exit Oystermouth Square

Estimated travel time: 2 hours 30 minutes

Nearby: Oystermouth Castle (1 min/ 500 ft away), Mumbles Pier (4 min/ 1.2 miles away), Mumbles Beach (3 min/ .7 miles away), Swansea Museum (11 min/ 4.6 miles away)

Between The Mumbles and Tenby: Kidwelly Castle, Llansteffan Castle and Laugharne Castle

The Mumbles to Tenby

There is plenty for the whole family to enjoy in the area and it has a high enough population that finding a room for rent may be easier, especially during high season.

How to get there:

- Car: M4 in Penllergaer from Mumbles Rd/ A4067, turn left onto Sketty Lane A4216 and then turn left onto Carmarthen Rd/A483. Follow signs for St. Clears, A48 and A40 to A477 then follow signs for Tenby, A477 and A478 to destination

- Estimated travel time: 1 hour 25 minutes

- Bus: 2/2A bus in Oystermouth Square to Swansea (21 min/ 15 stops), exit Bus Station (Stand W) at Stand N take bus T1 TrawsCymru/Carmarthen (57 min/ 6 stops), exit Bus Station (Bay 9) walk to Bay 5, take bus 322/Havenfordwest (40 min/ 21 stops) exit

Primary School, then take bus 381/Tenby (45 min/ 31 stops), exit South Parade Terminus Only

- Estimated travel time: 3 hours 20 minutes

Nearby: Folly Farms Adventure Park and Zoo (13 min/ 6.3 miles away), Manorbier Castle (14 min/ 5.9 miles away), Presipe Beach (near Manorbier), Carew Castle (14 min/ 6.7 miles away), Lamphey's Bishop Palace (17 min/ 8.3 miles away), Skrinkle Beach and Church Doors Beach (12 min/ 5.7 miles away), Pembroke Castle (19 min/ 11 miles away),

Tenby to St. Davids

The whole area between Tenby and St Davids is beautiful and has an abundance to offer. You cannot go wrong staying anywhere in the area between these two towns.

How to get there:

- Car: Follow Harding St to Greenhill Rd/ A4139, then take A478, A4115, A4075 and A40 to Nun St/A487

- Estimated travel time: 1 hour

- Train: Tenby/Swansea (10 min/ 2 stops), exit Kilgetty, walk to bus stop St Mary's Place, take bus 381 Withybush (44 min/ 18 stops), exit Bus Station, Stand 5 take bus T11 TrawsCymru Connect/Fishguard (48 min/ 28 stops), exit New Street Playground - you are at your destination

- Estimated travel time: 2 hours 9 minutes

- Bus: Upper Park Road (stop 1) bus 381/Withybush arrives every 60 minutes (1h 7min/ 36 stops), exit Bus Station, walk from stand 1 to stand 5, take bus T11 TrawsCymru Connect/Fishguard (48 min/ 28 stops), exit New Street Playground - you are at your destination

- Estimated travel time: 2 hours 11 minutes

- Nearby: St Davids Bishop's Palace (0), Coastal Path (0), Marloes for boat to Skomer Island (43 min/ 22 miles away)

St. Davids to Fishguard

Fishguard did not appeal to me, I would much rather stay in Cardigan. If it is hard to find a vacancy in the area, then Fishguard will do, since it is not far away.

How to get there:

- Car: Head north on Nun St/A487 towards The

Pebbles, turn right onto A4219, then left onto A40, take 2nd exit at Rafael roundabout onto the A487, then at next roundabout take the 2nd exit onto Main St - then you have arrived.

- Estimated travel time: 30 minutes
- Bus: New Street Playground stop take T11

TrawsCymru Connect/Fishguard (45 min/ 20 stops), exit Ffordd yr Efail (bay 2) you are at your destination

- Estimated travel time: 50 minutes
- Nearby: The Coast (0), Cardigan (30 min/ 19 miles away), Cilgerran Castle (31 min/ 19 miles away)

CAMPING

A n alternative to renting a room or a house is camping or glamping. A lot of camp-grounds are located within a twenty-minute drive from sights listed in this guide and some are easily accessible from the coastal hiking paths, which is great if you are walking Wales.

I have not camped in this country yet, but after

doing this research I now have an aching to rent a yurt and get back to nature.

Bell Tent Wales

8 Crompton Way, Ogmore-By-Sea
Bridgend, CF32 0PD
belltentwales.co.uk

Camping Brecon Beacons

Cwmdu Campsite
Crickhowell, NP8 1RU
campingbreconbeacons.com

Camping Wild Wales

AryMwny, Mwny Hwnt, Trefin, Haverfordwest
SA62 5AL
campingwildwales.co.uk

Cardiff Caravan Park

Pontcanna Fields, Cardiff, CF11 9XR
cardiffcaravanpark.co.uk

Castle Knights

Usk Castle
Monmouth Rd, Usk, NP15 1SD
castleknights.co.uk

Eco Camping Wales

Maes Eglwys Farms, Swansea SA9 1GS
ecocampingwales.com

Hidden Valley Yurts and Lake House
Lower Gly Farm, Llanishen, Chepstow, NP16 6QU
hiddenvalleyyurts.co.uk

Heritage Coast Campsite
Monknash, Cowbridge, CF71 7QQ
heritagecoastcampsite.com

Our Welsh Caravan and Camping
Hendre Ifan Goch Farm, Glynogwr, Blackmill, Bridgend
CF35 6EN
ourwelsh.co.uk

WEBSITES RECOMMENDED

Airbnb.com

My "go-to" accomodation sight for everywhere around the world, well, where it is accepted - is Airbnb. You can rent a room in someone's home or the whole property - so there is something for everyone. I have had great stays all throughout my travels in all price ranges.

There are a couple tips I suggest if you are only

renting a room: a lock on the bedroom door, access to the kitchen and a coffee maker and a mini-fridge in the room and if possible a private bathroom. The times that I have rented just the bedroom, I usually do not sleep well. You need to take in consideration that some people stay out clubbing until the wee hours of the morning and don't care that others are trying to sleep when they return. When you have an early morning flight the last thing you want is to hear some woman wearing high-heels walking down the tile hallway at 3am.

When you sign up with my link you will receive money off on your second stay, when your first meets Airbnb stay requirements. I too receive a credit, this is a win-win for both of us. I thank you in advance for using my link.

http://abnb.me/e/WYwRpTzsN4

Blackmountain.co.uk

Adventure activities such as: gorge adventures, clay pigion shooting, caving, archery, high level rope course and zip line.

Breconbeacons.org

Everything you need to know about all the national park trails, castles and mansion information, places to eat and stay and things to do in the area.

Cardiffparks.org.uk

Historical facts and everything you need to know about the parks in Cardiff.

Cadw.gov.wales

You will find information about each Cadw site, of course, but you will also find lodging information that is provided by Cadw (lodging is near sites, the majority are not physically located on property). You can also learn everything you want to know about Welsh history.

Castlewales.com

Great historical facts about each castle in Wales and pictures are included.

GowerSurfing.com

All things for surfing, including lessons and paddleboard rentals. Check out their website for information for Caswell Bay, Swansea and Rhossili Bay, Gower

Llangennith Surf School

If you have wanted to learn how to surf, why not see if this sport is for you.

surfschool.wsf.wales

Museum.wales

Everything "National Museum" can be found here: National Museum Cardiff, St Fagans National Museum of History, National Waterfront Museum, Big Pit National Coal Museum, National Slate Museum, National Wool Museum and National Roman Legion Museum.

Nationalexpress.co.uk

National Express operates bus service around the United Kingdom. Sophia Gardens is the main bus terminal in Cardiff and is located in Bute Park, west side near downtown (it's about a 10-15 minute walk to the castle).

Nationaltrust.org.uk

If you are interested in staying in some unique accomodations or perhaps would like to camp, you might just find what you are looking for here. For those of you who are hiking, they provide informaion on bothies and bunkhouses that are found along the trail.

- Bothy - simple accomodations with no electricity in remote locations
- Bunkhouses, camping barns and bunk barns - a more comfortable accomodation than a bothy

Pitchup.com

This website has a huge listing of campgrounds for the United Kingdom. Regardless if you are camping, glamping or needing a place to hook-up your caravan, you will find that perfect location here.

RidingWales.com

Want to ride a horse along the beautiful countryside or the beach? Wales Trekking and Riding Association has centres located all around Wales. This website will provide all the information you need to pick the right centre for location and riding desire.

Thebeachguide.co.uk/south-wales

This website has everything you need to know about beaches around the United Kingdom.

Uk.megabus.com

Mega Bus operates around the United Kingdom

and Europe.

VisitPembrokeshire.com

Tidbits of information about the Pembrokeshire area, including current events and upcoming.

Wales Online

A variety of information that has to do with anything and everything Wales, including camping sites.

AFTERWORD

Thank you for buying my guidebook. I hope it has shed some insight on the abundance Wales has to offer and you find it an ongoing reference during your travels.

Once upon a time, I was a blogger; while I chose not to continue that path, I do have stories available on my blog page and some photographs that I captured are up for sale on Fine Art America and Dreamstime. And like most travelers these days, I am also found on YouTube under A Traveler's Postcard.

atravelerspostcard.com
www.fineartamerica.com/profiles/paula-wheeler
www.dreamstime.com/
Pjwheeler_info#res7605434

Until the time comes for your Welsh experience,

have fun planning and I wish you a joyous journey. Wherever you may roam.

Happy Travels - P. J. Wheeler

ACKNOWLEDGE-MENT

All of the photos in this guide were taken by my-self, with the exception of the puffins. I would like to give thanks to Paul Edney for his contribution on Pixabay. You can check out his captures at: http://pixabay.com/photos/puffins-birds-nature-wildlife-5170165

My kids, grandson, parents and friends have been wonderfully supportive of my adventurous spirit, which I appreciate. It's emotionally challenging being away, so it's nice knowing they are cheering me on. The emails, calls and text keep me feeling connected and not so far away.

I would also like to give a huge thank you to my partner, without him driving me around the country every weekend, this book would not have been possible.

ABOUT THE AUTHOR

P. J. Wheeler

When P. J. Wheeler's children had grown-up and found their own path, she sold her possessions and left America to live life "out of her comfort zone." Having the motto "if we dream it, we can achieve it" - P.J. has been living the nomadic lifestyle since 2017 as a writer, photographer, videographer and travel consultant.  She finds joy in proving the media wrong; the world is not the scary place they want you to believe. It is filled with friendly citizens who take pride in their homeland and are happy to show it off.

REFERENCES

Aberglasney.org (2020)

Bmr.wales (2020)

Botanicalgardens.wales (2020)

Breconbeacons.org (2020)

Cadw.gov.wales (2020)

Cardiffbay.co.uk (2020)

Cardiffcastle.com (2020)

Cardiffparks.org.uk (2020)

Cardigancastle.com (2020)

Carewcastle.com (2020)

Castellhenllys.com (2020)

Dyfed-shires.co.uk (2020)

Dewstow Garden and Grotto.co.uk (2020)

Ewennypriory.co.uk (2020)

Folly-Farm.co.uk (2020)

gwili-railway.co.uk (2020)

Goape.co.uk (2020)

Google Maps (2020)

Llandaffcatherdral.org.uk (2020)

Llansteffancastle.com (2020)

Manorbiercastle.co.uk (2020)

Margamabbey.co.uk (2020)

Margamcountrypark.co.uk (2020)

Museum.wales (2020)

Nationalexpress.co.uk (2020)

Nationaltrust.org.uk (2020)

Newtheater.cardiff.co.uk (2020)

Pembrokecastle.co.uk (2020)

Pembrokeshireislands.co.uk (2020)

Pbrly.co.uk (2020)

Piers.org.uk (2020)

Royalmint.com (2020)

Showcaves.co.uk (2020)

Stdogmaelsabbey.org.uk (2020)

Swansea.gov.uk (2020)

Swanseamuseum.co.uk (2020)

Thebeachguide.co.uk/south-wales (2020)

Uskcastle.com (2020)

Valeofglamorgan.gov.uk (2020)

Visitmerthyr.co.uk (2020)

VisitPembrokeshire.com (2020)

VisitPembrokeshireCoast.Wales (2020)

Visitthevale.com (2020)

Visitwales.com (2020)

Vodafone.co.uk (2020)

Welshwildlife.org (2020)

Wmc.org.uk (2020)

Printed in Great Britain
by Amazon